THE
ETERNAL
COMPETITOR

Finding **Life** Beyond *the* Scoreboard

SCOTT W. SHUFORD

Col. 1:28-29

HIGH BRIDGE BOOKS
HOUSTON

The Eternal Competitor
by Scott Shuford

Printed in the United States of America
ISBN (Paperback): 978-1-946615-05-3
ISBN (eBook): 978-1-946615-06-0

High Bridge Books titles may be purchased in bulk for educational, business, fundraising, or sales promotional use. For information please contact High Bridge Books via www.HighBridgeBooks.com/contact.

Published in Houston, Texas by High Bridge Books

For my beautiful wife and our four champion boys.
Always keep your eyes up.

CONTENTS

FOREWORD

SO MANY TIMES, I have wondered, *Is there more?* These thoughts have been as shallow as wondering if there is another slice of a very good pizza or as deep and introspective as questioning if *this* is really all God intended for my life. These questions have forced me to look beyond the everyday fabric of the mundane and to lift my eyes in a search for something greater—something eternal.

In its purest form, a parable is the weaving together of everyday life events with God's truths. Through these practical stories, God wants us so desperately to connect the dots of His desires for us and how we live out our lives each day. *The Eternal Competitor* is a book that will help you connect those dots. On its best day, sports struggles not to be an idol. It wants to be worshiped by its coaches, athletes, parents, and fans. We must find out what it means to be an eternal competitor.

I have known Scott Shuford as an athlete, husband, father, and disciple who makes disciples. This work is an inspired read that draws on each of the roles God has brought Scott through over the years.

I am often asked about the influences in my careers as an athlete, coach, and leader. I always point to a mom who was committed to helping my brother and I to grow personally and spiritually and who never let sports become more important than who I was as person. I will also never forget a high school coach whose beliefs and behaviors matched every day. *The Eternal Competitor* enlightens parents and coaches to the real life-and-death decisions that surround this generation and serves as a guide book for the journey.

Reflection is always good. Through the personal stories and biblical application, this book creates the opportunity to see clearly where you are in your journey with sport as you fix your eyes on the eternal.

SHANE WILLIAMSON
President and CEO, Fellowship of Christian Athletes

ACKNOWLEDGMENTS

Shortly after graduating from college, God planted the vision for this book in my heart. Now, after nearly 10 years of God's faithfulness, the project is complete. There is no way to thank God for all of the incredible partners who made this work possible. It is for these amazing friends and helpers that I give thanks:

My Heavenly Father – Thank you for never giving up on me. You were so patient and so generous to continue to stoke the vision even over years of almost disobedient levels of dedication to the project. I am humbled to be your son and to be used in this way.

My amazing wife – You always see the best in me, and you never let me settle. Thank you for making me a better man. Thank you for standing beside me and speaking courage and life to me through this journey. None of this would be possible without you. I love you.

My boys – Thank you for giving Daddy the space to finish this book. Your bright eyes and teachable hearts give me hope that anything is possible. May you glean richly from God's truths within these pages and be strong competitors for Christ. I love you.

My parents – Thank you for always being there – through my athletic journey and through the adventure following. Your constant support and love have made me who I am today.

Dave Newell and Shane Williamson – Thank you for taking the time to read the rough draft and for giving me hope that this project was more than just a crazy dream. I love you both.

Todd Gongwer – Thank you for discipling me in the process of writing and leading. You are a true gift to me, and I look forward to what the future holds.

Georgia, Duncan, Lexie, Emily, Whitney, Adam, and Patrick – Thank you for your invaluable feedback and perspective on the book. *Many* changes were made because of your diligence. Keep changing the world!

Darren Shearer – Thank you for being so patient with me. Your grace and wisdom have been incredible gifts along the way. I praise God for crossing our paths through your father.

My coaches and teammates – I have learned much of what it means to be a man through watching your examples. Thank you for taking the time to care for me and teach me about life.

So many others – Your persistent prayers and timely encouragements were like water on the long, uphill journey. God used you so precisely, and I pray that you know how thankful I am for you.

1

THE SETUP

*Therefore we do not lose heart. Though outwardly we are wasting away, yet inwardly we are being renewed day by day. For our light and momentary troubles are achieving for us an eternal glory that far outweighs them all. **So we fix our eyes not on what is seen, but on what is unseen. For what is seen is temporary, but what is unseen is eternal.***

—2 CORINTHIANS 4:16-18

ONCE UPON A TIME, a man stepped into the batter's box, and with a looping, left-handed swing, he sent the pitcher's breaking ball over the right-field wall. His team won the game and, eventually, the series. And they all lived happily ever after. The end.

Great story, huh? Can't you just picture the scene? Can't you feel the intensity of the celebration as one swing cut through the pounding tension like a knife and settled everything that hung in the balance? I'll bet you can't wait to put this book down and go tell your momma, your neighbor, and your children's children the life-changing story of how somewhere, at some point in history, a guy hit a home run! Well... probably not.

While this "riveting" short story is probably not enough to make you run to your neighbor's house—much less, shift your position on the couch—I guarantee that, if you experienced the story at a deeper level, if you knew what was *really* going on, it would move you to at least consider sharing it with someone else. But without the details... without more than just the obvious facts... how can I expect you to be moved at all? "Where is the meaning? Where is the color, the life, and the passion?

Why should I even care?" you ask. Great questions! If you'll go with me, I would be delighted to take your surface-level knowledge of one of the greatest sports stories of all time and peel back the layers to show you that there's always more going on than what meets the eye.

To truly know the story, we must travel all the way back to October 15, 1988 to an afternoon matchup between the Oakland Athletics and the Los Angeles Dodgers. This was no sleepy, run-of-the-mill, mid-season game, however. This was Game One of the 1988 Major League Baseball World Series. And although this championship matchup featured such legends of the diamond as Orel Hershiser, Dennis Eckersley, José Canseco, and Mark McGwire, the hero of our story is found just outside their glow.

Kirk Gibson was an All-American football player at Michigan State who took his coach's advice and played baseball during his junior year for the sole purpose of putting pressure on the NFL teams who were looking to draft him the following fall.[1] Gibson's experiment in college baseball went so well that he was drafted in the first round by the Detroit Tigers in the spring of 1978. Turning down several lucrative offers from the NFL, Gibson traded his shoulder pads for a baseball bat and never looked back. In 1988, after nine years in the Tigers' organization, Gibson was picked up as a free agent by the Los Angeles Dodgers in a move that set the stage for one of the greatest home runs of all time.

Although Gibson led the team in '88 with 25 homers, him getting an at-bat in Game One of the World Series was, by all accounts, a miracle. In the N.L.C.S. leading up to the World Series, Gibson sprained his right knee and pulled his left hamstring while making a sliding, game-saving catch against the New York Mets. His legs were in such bad condition that, when the Dodgers won the series, manager Tommy Lasorda wouldn't even let him run out to the mound for the postgame celebration for fear that he would further injure himself.[2]

To make things worse—as if two bum legs weren't bad enough—the night before the World Series was slated to begin, Gibson had come down with a nasty stomach virus. His teammates described our hero on the day of the game as sickly and as steady on his feet as a "one-legged steer."[3] At this point, he's probably not matching the stud power-hitter you imagined when you first heard the story... is he?

Gibson showed up early to the ballpark that day, and after being carted from the parking lot to the locker room, he went about the business of trying to get ready to play that afternoon. As optimistic as he was, an injection to dull the throbbing tendon in his knee still left him limping around with near crippling pain. As the day progressed, the chances of Gibson contributing to the game grew smaller and smaller. After not even being able to make it out on the field for player introductions, he traded his uniform for a pair of blue Dodgers shorts and a "Michigan Big Game Hunter's Association" t-shirt and hobbled back to the training room to watch the game on T.V. and ice his legs.

At 3:04 p.m., seemingly oblivious to the fact that our main character was not even in uniform, Tim Belcher threw the first pitch in front of a near-capacity crowd of 55,983 at Dodger Stadium, and the 1988 World Series was underway. The Dodgers jumped out to a quick two-run lead before the heavy-hitting José Canseco hammered a ball out of the park for a grand slam to put the A's up 4-2. Both teams were kept from scoring again until the Dodgers strung together a few hits in the sixth to make the score 4-3 in favor of Oakland. While Gibson was removed from the action in the dugout, he wasn't immune to the mounting excitement and the growing possibility that the Dodgers could pull off the come-from-behind victory and that maybe, just maybe, he could play a part in it. He would later say in an interview that it was the TV announcer's proclamation that "Kirk Gibson's definitely not going to be available" that caused him to get up off the table, pull on his uniform, and set up the batting tee to see if the impossible could become reality.

At the top of the ninth, although wincing in pain, Gibson sent the bat boy to tell Coach Lasorda that he was available to pinch hit if they needed him. The excited Lasorda and our hobbling hero worked out a plan to hide him in the tunnel behind the dugout and then let him hit for the pitcher if they got there in the line-up.

The only problem with their plan was that the guy on the mound for Oakland was future Hall of Fame closer, Dennis Eckersley. Eckersley retired the first two batters, bringing the game within one out of an A's victory before issuing an uncharacteristic walk to the Dodgers' Mike Davis. This was just the break Lasorda and Gibson needed to put their plan into action. Lasorda pulled the light-hitting Dave Anderson he had been using as a decoy from the on-deck circle and sent Gibson limping up the steps instead. As he gritted his teeth, Gibson told himself that, once he heard the fans, his adrenaline would kick in and he'd be fine.

When the crowd at Dodger's stadium saw Gibson step out of the dugout with a bat in his hands, they let out a roar and exploded into a frenzy of excitement with the hope that their slugger could save the day. Even as Gibson gingerly approached the batter's box, you could see his confidence grow with the swell of the crowd. This was his time. This was the moment he had dreamed of and trained for his whole life. And now, against the greatest of odds, he stood toe to toe with destiny.

Eckersley knew Gibson was hurt and would have trouble catching up to the ball, so he decided to test him with a first-pitch fastball to the outside corner of the plate. Gibson fouled the ball off but nearly collapsed as his weight twisted onto his swollen knee. The second pitch was exactly like the first, an outside fastball that Gibson painfully fouled away to fall behind in the count 0-2.

After checking Davis at first, Eckersley delivered the 0-2 pitch, and Gibson chopped it down the first base line. Everyone in the stadium held their breath as Gibson limped down the base path after the ball that eventually rolled foul. "It had to be an effort to run *that* far," mused the TV announcer as Gibson again steadied himself at the plate.

Gibson took the next pitch for ball one, fouled the next one off and then watched as Eckersley sailed two more outside to bring the count to 3-2. To make matters worse for the A's ace, Davis had stolen second on his previous pitch, which meant Gibson only needed a base hit to tie the game and force extra innings.

So, there's the setup. It's Game One of the World Series, bottom of the ninth, two outs, full count, the Dodgers are down one with a runner on second, and Kirk Gibson is at the plate. Now, our story begins with a new perspective.

Once upon a time, a man stepped into the batter's box, and with a looping, left-handed swing, he sent the pitcher's breaking ball over the right-field wall. His team won the game and, eventually, the series. And they all lived happily ever after. The end.

Can you picture it now? Does knowing what's happening beneath the surface allow the story to move you on a deeper level? Like most things in life, if we know what's *really* happening, what's *truly* at stake, everything takes on a much greater significance.

Even deeper than that, what if we could see sports, competition, and all of life through God's eyes? Would knowing how deeply He moves through it all cause us to take a second look at things?

Maybe the world has it wrong. (That's a novel concept!) Maybe SportsCenter and the multi-million-dollar contracts don't necessarily reflect the true and deeper reality of what's happening in the world of sports. Maybe when the athlete meets God, He will have something more to say to him or her than things like, "What was your batting average? How much was your signing bonus?" Maybe God is more concerned with what we can't see, with what's happening on the inside, than He is with what the world marvels over.

A New Perspective

The Bible says over and over again that "The Kingdom of God (God's true and deep reality, where He is King) is near" and that this same Kingdom "is forcefully advancing" its way into every aspect of life (Mark 1:15; Matthew 11:12). But when we look at the Kingdom's closest adherents, very rarely do we see the same picture we see on the front of Sports Illustrated. Rather than being one of fortune, fame, and success, the picture is usually one of God's people joyfully embracing jail cells, beatings, and eventual death. Why is that? It seems that either God is wrong or that sport has been lured off the path by the glitz and glamour of what we see on the surface.

I am an athlete. I have played sports throughout my entire life. I currently serve as the Campus Director for the Fellowship of Christian Athletes at my alma mater, Furman University in Greenville, South Carolina and have spent nearly the last decade years struggling with exactly how and where God's Kingdom and the kingdom of sports collide. As I look back over my time in sports from little league to college football, there were times when the world would have called my teams and myself an undeniable success. However, the way I ended my career left many saying I had peaked three years earlier and left the game washed up. But what would God say? How would He view my career? From the three state championships to riding the bench my senior year of college? What is the true measure of success? What is He really up to? Does God even care about athletics?

I believe that one of the many frontlines of God's Kingdom runs squarely through every locker room, court, and playing field in the world. I have experienced God in some of the most incredible and tangible ways on "third and long" as well as when counting down the seconds on the way to a huge win. God is *alive*, and He is working mightily in the arena of sports! However, I believe that the true, *eternal* ways that He is moving are hidden beneath the surface of what the world focuses on. Because this is true, we all must answer this question—every guy and every girl—as we begin to examine sport, competition, and life through God's eyes: "What does it truly mean to be an eternal competitor?"

TRAINING TIME

1. How could the fact that God has a view of competition that differs from the world affect the way you live and compete?
2. What "hidden" part of your life do you wish those around you could see?
3. What do you think God has to say about the way you have viewed competition and athletics up to this point?

---

[1] http://sportsillustrated.cnn.com/vault/article/magazine/MAG1094754/index.htm

[2] http://sports.espn.go.com/espn/espn25/story?page=moments/3

[3] http://sports.espn.go.com/espn/espn25/story?page=moments/3

2

THE JOY OF PLAY

Rejoice in the Lord always. I will say it again: Rejoice!

—PHILIPPIANS 4:4

Truly I tell you, unless you change and become like little children, you will never enter the kingdom of heaven.

—MATTHEW 18:3

NEARLY EVERY NIGHT WHEN I GET HOME, I am met by three wild boys with one request: "We play dinosaur game, Daddy? We play dinosaur game… puhleeeeeeze?" After dozens of these appeals, I've perfected my response: I look down at the papers in my hand… Sigh… Look up at the ceiling… Drop my stuff on the floor… Smile at them… And do my best T-Rex impression. As soon as they realize that it's game on, they take off at full speed, literally squealing with glee. I don't know if you've ever played dinosaur game before, but the purpose of the game is for the tiny caveboys to escape being eaten/tickled by the big, hungry dinosaur. It's pretty serious! Once I catch a boy, I flip him up in the air and gnaw on his belly while he laughs until he turns blue. Occasionally, one of them will want to ride on my back while I chase the other two. I haven't exactly figured out what this has to do with dinosaurs, but it is obvious that they love it!

I can't remember all the way back to being two years old, but I'm pretty sure that my experiences were a lot like theirs, and I'll bet yours were, too. There isn't a preschooler out there who doesn't come alive at the prospect of being chased by a dinosaur, raced to the end of the driveway, or wrestling on the living room floor. There just seems to be something in the wiring of children that sees all competition as an opportunity to experience an explosion of joy. And if you don't believe me, drive to your nearest elementary school during recess, close your eyes, and get lost in the symphony of pure delight. We were built for that, but all too often, somewhere along the line, someone or something has tried to snuff out that flickering flame of joy we were all given by God.

The Joy of Play

Popsicle sticks on the old bus parking lot... That's about all I remember from my first, formal competition. It was first grade. It was fall. It was time for the mile run. I don't know why this memory is so vivid amongst the collage of the athletic experiences of my life, but it surely sticks out. Maybe it is because, having lived the majority of my life as a big, slow offensive lineman, it was the only time in my life when I remember being fast. I mean, like rocket-ship fast... racecar fast... faster than anyone else out there! Or maybe it is because of the pure joy I experienced as I circled that parking lot again and again, collecting a popsicle stick on each lap... in complete freedom and with my only goal being to run as fast as I possibly could for as long as I could.

I know that time softens and embellishes all memories, but I can't tell you the number of moments in my life when I have longed to drop everything and go back to the place where there were no standings, no critics, and where the only trophies involved were the wind in your hair, the burning in your legs, and the simple satisfactions that you gave your best.

This dream continued for me throughout the years of foursquare, field days, and backyard football games. Every time I competed in a three-legged race or made an interception as a free safety (my favorite backyard football position by far!), I truly believe I was experiencing the joy of sport in its purest form, exactly how God intended for it to be.

Love at First Sight

In third grade, I got my first football helmet. The time had come, and I was finally old enough to join the local youth league as a member of the Eastway Steelers. Yeah, Baby! It was like Christmas on steroids when they opened up the big, cinderblock press box to distribute the shoulder pads and helmets to the swarm of tiny football players who had assembled there. Seeing the vast array of helmets from the different teams, marveling in the piles of shoulder pads, and finally receiving my own hardware left me in awe of the beauty and great privilege that sport was unlocking in my life.

When I got home, I did what every other red-blooded kid who had just received his first football helmet would do. I grabbed my old blue bike, strapped on my shiny new headgear, and took off for a spin around the block to make the official announcement that "I was going to be playing football this year." For the first time in my life, I had been given the opportunity to take the joy of giving my all onto a new team and into a new arena. I had arrived!

I had played tee-ball, soccer, and basketball before, but nothing seemed to make me come alive like this newfound game of football. It was crazy. I loved my teammates. I loved getting to hit people. I loved the challenge of learning plays. I even loved the grinding and sweating of post-practice conditioning. It was like I had been ushered into a brand-new amusement park where every turn provided an exciting new challenge, adventure, and opportunity to do my best.

It wasn't always easy. I vividly remember getting continually bulldozed by future NFL linebacker Omar Gaither during that great rite of passage called "bull in the ring" and a particular football game that was so cold that I literally couldn't feel my fingers. But something deep inside of me found so much joy in putting it all on the line, pushing until I didn't have anything left, and striving for a goal together with my brothers on the team. I don't think I have ever been as free or had as much fun playing organized sports as I did during those three years with the Steelers, and I thank God for the opportunity to have been fully alive in that way.

However, as you can probably guess from my overly nostalgic long-ing to return to the simple joy of my Pee-Wee football days, my sports story did not continue along this same trajectory. As the years went by, pressures from the inside and outside did their best to steal my joy of sports, replacing it with fear, anxiety, bitterness, and pride.

I often wondered how this process began.

Where did the attack start?

What were the factors that played into crushing the child-like joy we all started with?

When I was in college, God gave me a front-row seat to the begin-ning of the process, and it nearly broke my heart.

Eyewitness to the Assault

I always wanted to be a baseball umpire.

I don't know much about the game. I'm not even really a diehard baseball fan. I just wanted to be the guy behind the plate with the power to call balls and strikes, and I was especially excited about choreo-graphing my own signature "punch-out" for called third strikes. It was a little selfish, I know, but it was one of those things I had always wanted to do. So I signed up at the local YMCA, bought a light-blue golf shirt from Old Navy with numbers on the sleeve, and began my career as an umpire for kid-pitch baseball and softball games.

It didn't take me long to realize that I wasn't cut out to be an um-pire. I had trouble remembering to click my ball/strike counter, my knowledge of the game's finer points was lacking, and I really didn't like getting yelled at by coaches and parents. However, I stuck it out and did my best because I had made a commitment to the league, and I really enjoyed getting to interact with the players.

Of the dozens of games I called that spring, one player sticks out from the rest because I was an eyewitness to a first-degree assault on his joy. The game was a classic matchup between the Braves and Yankees, but as soon as the teams walked up, I could tell it was going to be a mismatch. Every one of the Braves' 17 players was decked out from head to toe in the latest and greatest sports gear. They had wristbands on top of wristbands, and nearly every player had two bats in their customized baseball backpacks. They had three coaches on their staff, and the area behind the backstop was brimming with parents and siblings who were all wearing the team colors. Not only did the Braves look good, their pregame drills were as crisp as their uniforms. They were the real deal!

The Yankees couldn't have been more different.

Their dugout had two bags and three bats that the eight players shared amongst themselves. Their uniforms were blue t-shirts tucked into worn-out grey pants. Their cleats didn't match, and I honestly can't remember if they all had hats or not. Their coach was a young volunteer from the YMCA who I could tell cared deeply about the boys but wasn't overflowing with baseball strategy and knowhow. As the Yankees warmed up, a scattered handful of parents and passersby gathered to watch the David-and-Goliath moment that was getting ready to play itself out on the diamond.

True to form, the Braves scored ten runs in the top of the first and gave way to the Yankees at the plate. The first Yankee batter grounded out to short and trotted back to the dugout.

The next batter was the one who opened my eyes to the battle that was being waged beneath the surface of the game for the hearts of these tiny baseballers. The little Yankee bounced up to the plate, straightened his oversized helmet, dug his heals into the batter's box, and looked back at me. As we made eye contact, he gave me a cartoonish grin, winked at me, and said "Watch this!" With not an ounce of pride or spite in his four-foot frame, my heart couldn't help but root for this tiny slugger. Everything in me wanted him to hit a homerun that rolled into the woods 1,200 feet away. The simple purity of his joy and excitement is something I will never forget. What happened next is something I will never forget either.

As he turned around and focused on the pitcher, I could see his little knuckles tightening on the bat as every fiber of his being focused on smashing the incoming pitch. As the ball came in, he took a mighty swing. Strike one. As soon as the ball hit the catcher's mitt, a voice from my right side invaded the magical moment I was sharing with the competitors on the field. "Geeze! What the heck are you doing? Hit the dang ball, Jason!" Startled, I looked over at the bleachers to see a man in sunglasses and a button-up dress shirt with a disgusted look on his face. He shook his head and continued to mumble under his breath as his son squared back up in the box.

The second pitch was a ball, but it didn't appease his father. "Are you scared to swing now? *What* is the matter with you? Hit the ball!" As my focus returned to the little boy gripping the bat, I could see tears begin to form in the corners of his eyes. Every word from the stands seemed to make his grip tighter and tighter. Gone were the impish smile and twinkle in his eye. He now had the look of someone who was exerting great effort to stand up under excruciating pressure. As the pitcher wound up, my heart yearned for the boy in the box to be successful… for him to experience the fullness of the joy he brought to the plate with him. The pitch came in… Another big swing… Strike two. His father was livid. He stood up, grabbed the fence, and literally screamed at his son through the chain links.

As the fiery darts of his verbal barrage pounded the heart of his child, I directed my attention back to the batter. He was shaking violently now, huge tears were rolling down his cheeks, and I could hear him cry through gritted teeth, "Shut up, Dad… I hate you!" Needless to say, the next swing was miles behind the pitch, and as this tiny athlete made his way back to the dugout with his shoulders slumped, eyes down, and bat dragging behind him—and still being berated by his father—my mind flashed back to a video I had once seen where a lion attacked a young water buffalo. He chased him until he was cornered, swiped at him, and bit him until he couldn't stand anymore. He then violently ripped his throat out for the kill and carried his body away to devour it. While there was no blood to clean off home plate, I knew I had witnessed a very real attack, by a lion we will see more of later, on the pure and simple joy of sport.

Zero fun, Sir.

Coach Herman Boone: "You're smiling."

Petey Jones: "Yes."

Coach: "Yes, Sir? Why are you smiling?"

Petey: "Cause I love football! Football's fun."

Coach: "Fun, Sir? It's fun?"

Petey: "Yes."

Coach: "You sure?"

Petey: "I think…"

Coach: "Now you're thinkin'? First you smile. Then, you're
    thinkin'… You think football is still fun?"

Petey: "Uh, yes…"

Coach: Sir.

Petey: "Yes… No, Sir."

Coach: "No? It was fun. Not anymore, though, is it? Not
    right now. It's not fun anymore. Not even a little bit?"

Petey: "Uh… No."

Coach: "Make up your mind. Think since you're thinking.
    Go on. Think. Is it fun?"

Petey: "No, Sir."

Coach: "No? Absolutely not?"

Petey: "Zero fun, Sir."

While this exchange from the movie *Remember the Titans* is in no way meant to paint Coach Boone or his monumental achievements in any sort of negative light, it is, however, a prime example of how a coach's words—when expertly applied to just the right pressure points—can begin to steal the pure, simple joy of sport from his or her players. Far from being just a theory, I have firsthand experience with the negative power of a coach's words.

I will be the first to admit that I don't have the sharpest long-term memory in the world. Years of repetitive head banging on the O-line has left me somewhat cloudy on any memories that don't have an associated picture in our photo albums. I imagine this is the case for a lot of us, but it doesn't change the fact that our memories—real or altered—have the power to shape our understanding of ourselves and the world around us. With that being said, I don't remember *everything* from my junior year of high school football, but I do remember this:

"Shuford, *you* suck."

"Shuford, that was *terrible*."

"What were you thinking?"

Those were the only words that my head coach leveled at me... all year long.

On one particular Friday night, I was struggling to keep my guy out of the backfield. I remember it well. He was a tall, quick, athletic defensive end, and his red #40 jersey still haunts me... not so much for what he did to me on the field but for what my coach did in response.

Halfway through the second quarter, as we stood in the huddle awaiting our direction, I heard Coach yell, "Hey, Shuford!" It had always been quiet when we played at this school, but for some reason, you could hear a pin drop in the stadium as Coach bellowed out my name. I turned to look at him on the sidelines and his pointing finger toward me. His look of disgust burrowed into my soul as he shouted the rest of his declaration: "You suck!" Stunned and saddened, I tried to regain my composure. After a halftime of staring blankly through my facemask, I did, in fact, have a much improved second half. But something in my heart had started to die. If you had run a test on me that evening, I guarantee you would have been hard pressed to find any traces of the joy that had led me to the game some eight years earlier.

As the season wore on, I continued to wonder how I had gotten to where I was. I mean, I was just a normal 16-year-old kid who loved to push myself, loved the game of football, and wanted to be a part of something bigger than myself. I worked hard, took care of my school work, and led to the best of my abilities. But it didn't seem to matter. Nothing I did was ever good enough for Coach. Even though we were defending state champs, hadn't lost a game since the beginning of the previous season, and I was a two-year starter on the varsity team, my joy was dead. Not only was it dead, it was being continually spit on and kicked by a coach who seemed determined to make sure it stayed that way.

Recently, as I was recounting the damaging verbal assaults of my junior season, my wife Jess stopped me and said, "You know that's the year your Mom died, right?" I was floored. For some reason, I had never put two and two together and realized that this attack had come at the weakest, most vulnerable point of my life. There are two things I realized at that moment.

First, every coach has a monumental responsibility in the lives of his or her players. When my life was caving in and I was literally watching my mom die before my eyes, I *needed* my coach. I didn't need a lot. I just needed him to put his arm around my shoulders and tell me he was in my corner. There is no telling how that simple act of love would have changed my life and path. God has created the position of coach to speak directly into the hearts and lives of the young people with whom they have been entrusted. It is the coach's choice whether to speak life or speak death.

Second, Satan loves to kick you when you are down. He is crafty and hell-bent on doing everything in his power to slide in at just the right moment when your defenses are down and plant a bomb with the hopes of derailing every hope and dream God has for you. There are no lengths to which he will not go to try to destroy what God is building. Jesus is greater, and Satan has ultimately been defeated, but that does not mean we can drop our gloves and pretend that the war is over.

I started high school as an eager, joyful 14-year old who loved every aspect of the game of football. I loved being a part of the team and even relished in the conditioning and long practices. My life was simple, and my joy was intact. I finished high school as a three-time state champion, a varsity record of 43-1, a two-time All-State selection, a three-year starter, and a college football scholarship in hand. But my joy—one of the main reasons I played the game—had been seriously wounded, and scars of fear, worry, and doubt had begun to creep across my soul.

The Hidden War

I don't know if you realize it or not, but you and I are in the middle of a war. Just below the surface of everyday life, a vicious battle is raging for the hearts, minds, and souls of every human being on planet Earth. From the beginning to the end, the Bible is clear that there is an enemy who stands in direct opposition to God and to His people and purposes. Jesus says that His enemy, Satan, is "the father of lies" and that he exists only to steal, kill, destroy, and launch accusations at everyone on planet Earth (John 8:44; John 10:10; Revelation 12:10). The Bible even says that Satan "prowls around like a roaring lion looking for those that he can [pin down, rip their heart out, and] devour" (1 Peter 5:8). *The Message* Bible puts it this way:

> This is no afternoon athletic contest that we'll walk away from and forget about in a couple of hours. This is for keeps, a life-or-death fight to the finish against the Devil and all his angels. Be prepared. You're up against far more than you can handle on your own. (Ephesians 6:10-12)

Without Jesus, we would be as helpless as a kindergartener trying to escape from a 500-pound lion. We wouldn't stand a chance. Fortunately for us, God sent His Son Jesus to wage war against the enemy of all mankind. When Jesus began His ministry, He was tempted by Satan. But unlike Adam and Eve in the Garden (and all of us alive today), He resisted the attacks of the enemy and sent him packing. Jesus ultimately defeated, de-fanged, and de-clawed Satan by sacrificing His life on the cross, dying, and then storming back to life, showing once and for all that the enemy's greatest weapons of sin and death are powerless to hold God down. I love how Paul puts it in his letter to one of the local churches:

> When you were dead in your sins… God made you alive with Christ. He forgave us all our sins, having canceled the charge of our legal indebtedness, which stood against us and condemned us; he has taken it away, nailing it to the cross. *And having disarmed the powers and authorities, he made a public spectacle of them, triumphing over them by the cross.* (Colossians 2:13-15)

Did you hear that? He didn't just barely squeak by. He completely disarmed and destroyed the power of the enemy and did it in a public and humiliating way. Talk about *power!*

The good news is that Jesus is stronger than Satan. He has forgiven *all* sin and has defeated death forever. If we give everything to Him and allow Him to help us build our lives on what He has done on our behalf, we will be able to walk in victory over anything that the enemy throws our way.

The bad news is that Satan still thinks that he can win, and he is constantly engaging in the war with as much tenacity as he can muster. He desires to lure everyone away and to kill the work of God in their lives. He hates God and the way He has created us to walk in relationship with Him, and he will use everything in his power to sidetrack, distract, discourage, and destroy all of humanity. Does that mean that he could use coaches, fathers, our work, and even sports to accomplish his task? Absolutely.

What if there is more to life than just what meets the eye? What if sport and true victory have more to do with the development of the heart than the padding of the stat sheet? What if coaches cared more for their players than their winning percentages? What would it look like to peel back the thick, rotten layers that our sports culture has draped over the pure joy of play that the Creator of the Universe has put in each of us?

J-O-Y, Joy!

I have been led to believe many lies: To be a true competitor, you must leave joy on the playground. Anxiety, worry, and doubt are natural and even necessary parts of competition. Fear of failure should be our greatest motivator.

The answer lies in a concept that is not foreign to the lives of many in the Bible: Joy.

Moses called God's people to serve God joyfully (Deuteronomy 28:47).

Nehemiah led the Israelites to rebuild the wall around Jerusalem by encouraging them to let the "joy of the Lord" be their strength (Nehemiah 8:10).

King David used the word *joy* 57 times in the book of *Psalms*.

Jesus taught His disciples that His desire was for His *joy* to be in them and that their joy would be complete (John 15:11).

Paul urged the Christians in Philippi to "rejoice in the Lord always" and reminded Timothy that God has "richly provided us everything for our enjoyment" (Philippians 4:4; 1 Timothy 6:17).

James teaches us to "consider it pure joy when we face trials of many kinds" (James 1:2).

Finally, the book of *Revelation* tells us that, one day, we will rejoice and be glad because Jesus is going to come back, throw a huge party, and "take His people in marriage like a bride" (Revelation 19:7). Just think of the greatest wedding reception you have ever been to, and multiply it by a million!

Joy is supported, celebrated, and encouraged throughout the Scriptures. As people who have been rescued from the penalty and slavery of our sin and restored into the light and a life-giving relationship with the God of all creation, our lives should be overflowing with a deep abundance of joy… not just bubbly, goofy happiness but a deep, lasting, joyful attitude of the heart that transcends all our circumstances. This is the same joy with which Jesus embraced the cross. The world didn't give it to Him, and the world sure couldn't take it away. Whether we are working, resting, or competing, this joy should extend from the security and beauty of our relationship with God into *every* area of our existence.

Anxiety, doubt, fear, worry, and a lack of joy all come from the same root issue: lack of faith.

I can vividly remember going up in a hot-air balloon at a local fair when I was younger. Mom and I paid for our tickets and stepped into the basket that was dangling below the massive balloon. I've never been a fan of heights. As the balloon started to rise, I noticed that the side of the basket—at least, in my mind—only came up to my waist. Fearing I was going to plummet to my death, I started to freak out. It was everything I could do to maintain my composure until the balloon landed back on the grass. My lack of faith in the basket sucked all the joy out of what should have been a wonderful, once-in-a-lifetime experience.

Although lack of faith breeds fear and anxiety, perfect love drives them out and creates an environment where joy can thrive (1 John 4:18).

Joy in Action

Recently, I was talking with one of my former college teammates about the football team he is coaching. He had just finished his first full year with the program and had seen a dramatic improvement in the performance of the team since he took over. When I asked him what was different about the approach he had been taking with the team, he told me that he and his coaching staff set an intentional focus on making sure that every boy in the program knew he was loved and how valuable he was as a young man. The results have been incredible! When he first walked into the program, the players were dominated by fear and lacked any joy or self-confidence. They did only what they were required to do and never took any risks for fear of failing. As my former teammate unleashed his program of love, family, and acceptance, the players blossomed into the young men they were created to be. Talk about a recipe for banishing the fear-dominated culture of sports and inviting back in the simple joy of giving your all, laying it on the line, and spending yourself for a cause greater than yourself!

You may not be on my buddy's high school football team, but if you have given your life to Christ and trusted Him as your Savior, you are on God's team. As you learn to place your faith in Him, anxiety, fear, doubt, and worry will begin to lose their death grip on your soul. As you realize how perfectly He loves you and how He has already gone to the greatest measures possible to demonstrate His love through Jesus' death on the cross, you will be freed up to live, compete, strive, and strain for things you never thought were achievable. You'll experience the freedom to fall down, get up, and try again because your identity, value, and worth as a person are not based on your performance or anyone else's evaluation of it. You are secure in Christ.

God's perfect love drives out all fear, anxiety, and worry while replacing them with His perfect joy. You only must choose to believe!

TRAINING TIME

1. Think of the time when you felt most free in the arena of competition. Why did you experience such great freedom in that moment?
2. Describe a time when your joy was attacked. What was the result of the experience?
3. How can knowing that you are in a life-or-death fight against the enemy of your soul help you to win the battle of joy? In what ways can God's Word equip you for the fight?
4. What application of the truths of this chapter do you want to make in your life?

3

WHAT HAPPENS WHEN YOU LOSE?

And we know that in all things God works for the good of those who love him, who have been called according to his purpose. For those God foreknew he also predestined to be conformed to the image of his Son, that he might be the firstborn among many brothers and sisters.

—ROMANS 8:28-29

For I know the plans I have for you, declares the LORD, plans to prosper you and not to harm you, plans to give you hope and a future. Then you will call on me and come and pray to me, and I will listen to you. You will seek me and find me when you seek me with all your heart.

—JEREMIAH 29:11-13

PANIC AND A DEEP SORROW STARTED TO RISE in my gut as I traced my finger down the list of names. After I reached the bottom of the page for the fourth time, reality began to set in… I had been cut. Standing there alone in the dimly lit hallway outside of Coach's office, my mind wandered back to my first baseball glove, my first homerun, and the hours that Dad and I had spent playing catch in the street. From tee-ball to kid pitch to little league, baseball had always been a special part of my life. While I was no diehard baseball junkie, I loved the game. If I had a dollar for each hour I spent watching Braves' games, categorizing my extensive baseball card collection, or tossing the ball around, I would be a rich man! There was something beautiful about the way the team dynamics danced with the personal responsibility at the plate and in the field that seemed to resonate deep in my heart. Add in the vast expanse of the sky in the outfield, the smell of peanuts, and the cracker jacks... I was hooked!

Some of my greatest memories with my Dad revolved around baseball. Whether we were working on ground balls at the park, throwing it around in front of the house, or fine tuning my pitching, there was always something special about the hours we spent together with that little leather ball.

On one occasion, Dad thought it would be a good idea to set up his car as a backstop while I worked on my fastball in the front yard. Even though I warned him (only halfway joking!) that he was going to have trouble catching up to my heater if it got away from me, he insisted that he would catch it and that the car would be fine. I shrugged and started going to work. A few minutes later, I let one go that tailed up and over Dad's mitt. We both watched with wide eyes as our beloved baseball shattered his rear driver's-side window and came to rest in the back seat. As I turned to run, Dad laughed and said, "Well... I guess you were right!"

As I continued to stagger from the realization that I had not made the team, something deep within me knew that, for me, baseball was over. I had already had trouble hitting the "real" pitches I had seen in little league, and I knew in my heart that this middle school tryout was my last shot. I had all but made a deal with myself that, if I didn't make the team, I was going to hang up the spikes for good. I thought I had had a great tryout. I knew I wasn't the most talented guy on the field, but I had hit several balls that rolled all the way to the school driveway behind the fenceless baseball field and had even strained my quad hustling to beat out a ground ball. I had laid it all on the line. I had given it everything I had. I had done my very best... and I had failed.

Just like awkwardness at a middle school dance, the distinctive smell of a high school football locker room, and gravity, there is one constant in life and in sport: *failure*. The greatest baseball hitter of all time only managed to hit the ball one out of every three times at the plate. The winningest college football team has lost 325 games over its

135-year history. Even Lebron James lost twice in the NBA finals before he finally won it all. Failures will come, but our challenge and God's calling is for us to see them through the eyes of the one who stands in control of everything, enabling us to discover the unseen eternal picture being painted underneath the surface.

The Root of Failure

When God created the heavens and the earth, He said, "It is *good*." There was no sin, no brokenness, no car wrecks, and no cancer. And I'll bet Adam and Eve had more hole-in-ones than Tiger Woods ever dreamed about. By God's design, everything was perfect. Failure and loss were not a part of the equation. Everyone and everything was un-defeated. God had created Adam and Eve in His image, and they were doing an incredible job working the land and taking care of the animals. He even walked with them and talked with them face to face in the cool of the evening. Everything was flowing along according to plan until our earliest ancestors made a choice that would alter the course of life as we know it.

Humanity did not continue on the original trajectory God intended for us. Sin derailed the human race. The Bible puts the story like this...

God intentionally and lovingly made man and woman in His own image. He placed them in a beautiful garden and gave them everything they needed to thrive. He gave them a clear purpose and invited them to partner with Him in taking care of the land and the animals. He pursued them, and they enjoyed an intimate, face-to-face, life-giving relationship with Him. He gave them only *one* restriction. They were not to eat fruit from one particular tree in the garden. Man was lured in by a sneaky curveball from Satan and made the intentional choice to disobey God. This act of intentional defiance drove a wedge between a now sinful man and a perfect God. God drove Adam and Eve out of the garden and told them that the rest of their lives would be filled with painful labor, sweaty toil, and unfulfilled desires.

In only one chapter, the story of humanity's fall goes from eating a piece of forbidden produce to a man jealously killing his own brother (Genesis 3-4).

Just two chapters later, God "saw how great the wickedness of the human race had become on the earth, and that every inclination of the thoughts of the human heart was only evil all the time." His heart was so deeply troubled that He destroyed everything and started over with the family of the only righteous man He could find (Genesis 6:5).

In the life of King David, we see a man who literally broke every single one of the Ten Commandments in his love affair with Bathsheba (2 Samuel 11).

The drunkenness, incest, idol worship, hatred, and sexual immorality of people described in the New Testament led Paul to say that "all have sinned and fallen short of the glory of God" (Romans 3:23).

When the first humans chose to disobey God, they invited sin into the picture. It may have seemed like a small thing to them at the time, but they unknowingly started an epidemic that would spread like cancer across the globe. Everywhere sin went, the kingdom of Satan went with it. So now, instead of finding themselves in the heart of a gracious Kingdom ruled by a loving King, Adam and Eve found themselves on the frontlines of a life-or-death battle between the kingdom of Satan and the Kingdom of the God Who created them.

This is exactly where we find ourselves. The world we live in today is a far cry from the way God intended for it to be. Sin has poisoned so badly everything that God designed that even "creation has been groaning as in the pains of childbirth" (Romans 8:22). Just one glance at the evening news drives this point home so clearly that it might make you want to hide under your pillow.

It is within this framework of brokenness that we now live and compete. No longer does every Cinderella story pan out, every swing produce a home run, or every Hail Mary find its intended receiver. The landscape of sports is so littered with scandals, slumps, season-ending injuries, failed playoff bids, and postgame brawls that it is impossible to ignore the effects that eating one piece of fruit had on every game, every coach, and every athlete. Every aspect of our world, including our sports culture, is desperately broken. It should come as no surprise that Jesus—who was homeless, harassed, tortured, and executed—would say, "In this world you will have trouble" (John 16:33).

The Fight of My Life

Shortly before my eleventh birthday, we heard the word no family ever wants to hear: *cancer*. Mom found a lump, and after a series of tests, she was diagnosed with breast cancer. As a 10-year-old boy, this news was staggering. I just knew Momma was going to die. I had never heard of anyone surviving cancer, only the sad tales of those who had fought it to the death. I remember lying in my bed and crying my eyes out as I begged the God I had heard about at church to do something. I had learned that He was big and that He could do anything that He wanted, so I figured it was a good idea to reach out to Him so He would heal my mom.

After months of intense treatment and fervent prayer, Mom's cancer was gone! I hugged Mom, thanked God wholeheartedly, made a note on what to do in case I ever needed God's help again, and went about my life.

Months later, Mom's cancer came back in a different spot. Strangely enough, as gut-wrenching as the first round was, the second one was incredibly easy. I took the lesson I had learned the first time—that God hears the prayers of His children and that He is more than happy to deliver the desired outcome—and applied it to my new situation. In what I would have called a true display of faith at the time, I tossed the situation up to the God I had heard was in control of everything and went on about my life. I was confident that, because I was a good kid and had reached out to Him about this, He would take care of it, and everything would be fine. And I was right! Mom was cancer-free again a few months later, and life returned back to normal.

This "genie-in-a-lamp" approach to God continued for the next three years until the summer before my junior year of high school. I remember coming home from football practice in July and seeing the looks on my dad's and brother's faces as I walked into the room. Dad told me

I needed to call Mom right away because she had something she wanted to tell me.

As the phone connected to the outpatient facility where she and my grandmother were staying during her second bone marrow transplant at Duke University Medical Hospital, my stomach sank. As always, the voice on the other end of the line was reassuring and full of life. Mom always had a way of finding the silver lining and highlighting the good in any situation. Even as she told me there were no more treatment options for her cancer and that she was coming home to spend her last days with Dad, my brother, and me, the deep peace she conveyed over the phone ministered to my soul.

The next six months were full of joy and heartache as my once beautiful, strong, and vibrant mother finished her grueling, six-year battle against this deadly disease. A simple walk around the block and a meal together at the dinner table became moments to treasure during the few precious remaining days we had together.

Christmas was wonderful. On New Year's Eve, Dad and Mom went out to dinner. On January 5, 2002, at 48 years old, Joan Shuford's epic struggle against cancer ended. The final score was Cancer, 1; Mom, 0... or so it seemed.

The TRUE Scoreboard

The world is always trying to make judgment calls. Everyone wants to sort people and experiences into neat, clean categories. Nowhere is this clearer than in the world of sports. If you have more points at the end of the game, you are a winner. If you didn't cross the finish line first, you are a loser. If you made the all-star team, you are a winner. If you got cut from the team, you are a loser. If your team goes 11-0, you are winners. If your team fails to win a single match, you are losers.

From our very first tee-ball game to the World Cup, everything around us promotes the idea that success is everything and that winning should be our only goal. If you are a winner, you must be doing something right. And if you are a loser, you must be doing something wrong.

In our culture, successes are signs of achievement and greatness to be dwelled on and memorialized in trophy cases for generations to come. Losses are shameful failures to be hidden away and forgotten about as quickly as possible. The problem with this model is that it is one-dimensional, and it doesn't allow us to make sense of the times when things don't work out. It only takes into account what you see on the outside. It ignores the reality that there is always more going on than simply what the box score shows. It dismisses the fact that these "embarrassing" loses can actually be some of the greatest moments of our lives... if we will let them.

You are NOT in control.

Looking back, it is clear to me that I had again fallen victim to lies from the world around me: I am in control of the outcome when I compete. If I am really following God, life is supposed to be easy, and everything will go my way. My failures are shameful and are to be hidden, forgotten, and avoided at all costs.

If there is one thing that my mom's journey with cancer made clear, it was the fact that you are not completely in control of the outcome of any part of your life. Even if you change your diet, have a positive outlook, and follow the doctor's orders perfectly, you can still end up on the losing end of the match. While the sports and marketing worlds seem to want you to believe that you can guarantee victory if you will drink the right sports drink, wear the right shoes, and follow the right workout regimen, reality seems to tell us otherwise.

On what happened to be my eighth birthday, Shaquille O'Neal and the Orlando Magic made the trek north to take on Michael Jordan and the storied Chicago Bulls. It was a night for the record books. Michael Jordan put forth an otherworldly effort, scoring 64 points on 49 shots from the floor. He was all over the court and doing everything in his power to will his team to victory. However, even though there are only six human beings on the planet who have scored more than 64 points in an NBA game, Michael and Bulls walked away from the game as losers.[1]

At the end of overtime, the scoreboard read 128 – 124 in favor of the visiting Magic.

Unfortunately for Michael, the game versus the Magic was five-on-five, not one-on-one. He could have matched up against any individual player on the other team—actually, any *two* players for that matter!—and still have scored more points than them, but the reality of the game was that it involved a lot more than just him. At any given time, there were four other Bulls and five opposing players on the court. We also must take into account that there were three men in striped shirts with whistles officiating the game, two coaches commanding the teams, and 18,000+ screaming fans in attendance.[2]

Even if you're Michael Jordan, you are not in complete control of the outcome of the game. Even if you have one of the most dominant performances of all time, there are still a host of other things that must fall into place in order for the scoreboard to go your way. So, what *can* we control?

The only thing you can control is yourself. God's call is for maximum *effort* and a Christ-like *attitude* every time you step into the arena of competition. What happens on the scoreboard is simply a byproduct of the sum of all the factors in the equation. You can't control the way the ball bounces; you can only control how hard you run after it! Do your best, and commit the rest to Him.

If we are not in control, as Christians, we must believe that God is. People often ask if God cares who wins a particular game, and I have heard it answered that God cares because He cares about the people who are competing. I like that because it rings true with the fact that God is intimately involved and deeply invested—at the cost of His own Son's life—in the lives of every coach, athlete, and human being on the planet. Does this mean that He blocks field goals, bends home runs around the foul pole, or causes quarterbacks to slip on the one-yard line? I'm not sure of those answers, but I do know that nothing is outside of His power! I believe the bigger point is that the God who created the Universe has the whole world in His hands and that He is able and willing to work "all things [even basketball games] together for the good of those who love Him and who are called according to His purposes" (Romans 8:28).

God doesn't make mistakes. He knows exactly what He is up to and has an amazing ability to weave the experiences of your life together to achieve His desired outcome. Win, lose, or draw, the Bible makes it clear that God sits enthroned over every circumstance and has a perfect plan to use it in the lives of those involved… if they will only listen.

Easy Street?

One of the most dangerous lies I have seen floating around out there is the belief that, if we honor God with our lives and possessions, everything will work out the way we want it to. It's a lie that life as a Christian is supposed to be easy. We are tempted to believe, just like coaches so often tell us, that if we "work harder" in our Christian lives—that is, if we read more, pray more, and give more—we will "win" more and that our lives will consist of one victory party after the other. While God does take care of His children and while there are incredible spiritual benefits that result from pursuing God with the right motive of deepening our relationship with Him, the real danger in this lie comes when things don't work out. If you are following this mode of thinking and things start to go south (e.g. you lose your starting spot, tear an ACL, don't win a match all year), there are two things you could start to assume.

First, you might assume you're not doing enough of the right things and must work harder to earn the good things God has stored up for you.

Second, you might assume God must not be who He said He is, that He must not love you, that He is too weak to impact your life, or that He must not even be real.

Think of it this way… You are the starting second baseman on the school's varsity baseball team. You had a great freshman season, but now, you find yourself in the depths of a sophomore-year slump. You can't hit anything at the plate, and it's starting to affect your confidence in the field. It's like every opposing pitcher has your number, and it seems like you can't do *anything* right in the box. Your first tendency is to get in the cage and grind out batting practice until your fingers bleed. You reexamine your stance, your grip, your timing, your follow through, and everything else you can think of to stop the downward spiral. While all the fine-tuning serves to focus you, it also begins to unnerve you when it doesn't produce results at the plate. You become so consumed with doing everything perfectly that the natural beauty of your swing is replaced by a choppy, pieced-together sequence of movements that is only able to produce a few fouls balls and a handful of popups.

To make matters worse, you start to question your coach, and your once-healthy relationship with him breaks down. You think... Maybe it's *his* fault. Maybe *he's* been teaching you the wrong technique the whole time. Maybe you'd be better off transferring to a different school to play for a coach who could really help you get out of this slump. Maybe you should just try to do it your own way. Maybe you should just quit baseball altogether.

We don't need to look any further than the lives of the twelve men who followed Jesus the closest to see that this way of thinking does not line up with the reality of the Bible. Ten of the twelve disciples were murdered because of their faith in Jesus. They were cut in half, crucified, stoned, hanged, and burned. The eleventh one didn't die when they threw him in a pot of boiling oil, so he was banished to a tiny island to die alone. In addition to their hardships, Paul, the author of much of the New Testament, was shipwrecked, beaten with rods, pelted with stones, often cold and naked, regularly without food and water, and in danger wherever he went (2 Corinthians 11:16-33). I am so glad they didn't view these "losses" as evidence that God had abandoned them and then decide to stop believing in Him. On the contrary, their hardships pushed them closer to God and gave them even more reason to rely on His unfailing goodness. They pressed on because they knew that Jesus spoke the truth when He said that this world is full of trouble (John 16:33). They knew God was in control and that sorrow, hardship, and loss were expected parts of the journey as He led them up the narrow path of becoming more like His Son Jesus.

Get back up!

One day while I was driving through the back of our neighborhood, I saw something I will never forget. Three coaches and a dozen or so boys with their heads and shoulders adorned with the armor of pee-wee football were working through a drill on the old ball field. The boys were lined up, one behind the other, about five yards from the first coach. The second coach was five yards behind the first, and both had blocking dummies in their hands. On the sound of the whistle, a boy would run as hard as he could toward the first coach, and the coach would knock him down with the blocking dummy. The boy would scramble to his feet and launch himself at the second coach, only to be knocked down again. He would fight his way back to a standing position and sprint through the line to end the drill. As I sat there and watched boy after boy make his way through the gauntlet the coaches had set up, I realized what they were doing. They were learning *how to get up*.

There is one guarantee in the game of life: you *will* get knocked down. There will be things that don't go the way that you planned. Things will break, people will let you down, and your best will not measure up to the world's standard. You *will* find yourself flat on your back, sucking wind, trying to make the clouds stop spinning, and picking grass out of your teeth. At that moment, you will have a choice to make. You can start crying, curl up in a ball, and wait for someone to come pick you up and take you home. Or, you can clear your head, grit your teeth, fight back to your feet, and keep running. The first response assumes that what is happening to you is unexpected, bigger than you can handle, and a good reason to quit. The second response sees the setback as a natural part of the game, an opportunity to dig deep and overcome, and a chance to learn and grow.

The choice is real: fight or quit. Every day, we are faced with this simple decision, and I believe that the role we will be allowed to play on God's team will be a direct result of how we consistently answer this question.

Winston Churchill said it well: "Success is not final. Failure is not fatal. It is the courage to continue that counts."[3] Paul put it this way in his letter to the Philippians:

> But one thing I do: Forgetting what is behind and straining toward what is ahead, I press on toward the goal to win the prize for which God has called me heavenward in Christ Jesus. (Philippians 3:13-14)

No matter how you get there, the call is simple: "Get up and keep running!" I have to believe that, just like those pee-wee football coaches, God's desire is to see how quickly we can trust the hope that He offers us, pick ourselves up off the ground, and keep putting one foot in front of the other.

He will use it.

A couple of years back, I asked my Dad a question I had always wanted to know the answer to but never had thought to ask. "Hey, Dad... Tell me about how your relationship with God began. What got you to where you are with your faith today?"

He said, "Well, the single biggest moment in my faith journey was when your mom died. I had been around people who died before, but the grace and peace that your mom had as she finished her time here on Earth proved to me, once and for all, that we can truly trust God with our lives *and* our deaths."

I wasn't necessarily shocked by his answer because my life had been forever impacted by the same truth when Momma left. But the depth of the reality that he revealed through his answer has never left me.

There is an eternal truth that God desires to teach us through every situation. If we will truly listen and let Him do the hard work of peeling back the layers of *every* part of our story—especially the tough times of failure and loss—this truth will transform us.

We will explore this in more depth later, but God is the greatest coach in the Universe, and He handcrafts every "drill" that He puts us through on this practice field called life. He knows exactly what parts of our game need improvement. Because He so desires for us to walk in the freedom and life that Jesus modeled, He lovingly uses every circumstance to make us like Him.

Just like in "real life," however, this doesn't mean that every drill or scrimmage situation He puts us through is fun or easy. I can remember several times during my two years on the high school wrestling team when I wanted to cry, throw-up, and pass out at the same time. But it is those times that have shaped me into the man I am today. Once you lose 13 pounds of sweat in one practice, changing diapers at 2:00 a.m. doesn't seem so bad!

I am not intending to downplay the difficult things we go through in life. We have all faced or will face seasons of loss and failure that are absolutely devastating. We will lose things and people we hold close to our heart. In those seasons of loss, it is only appropriate and even healthy that we would grieve and mourn the loss of the loved one, the job, the place on the team, the starting position, or the season we held so dear. It seems the harder you have fought for something and the more of yourself you have invested in the pursuit, the harder it is to swallow when it doesn't pan out the way you thought it should. But it is in exactly these moments when God's truth rings the most true.

> Therefore we do not lose heart. Though outwardly we are wasting away, yet inwardly we are being renewed day by day. For our light and momentary troubles are achieving for us an eternal glory that far outweighs them all. So we fix our eyes not on what is seen, but on what is unseen, since what is seen is temporary, but what is unseen is eternal. (2 Corinthians 4:16-18)

__TRAINING TIME__

1. What has been the greatest tragedy or defeat you have faced in life? How did that tragedy or loss change you?
2. What do you want to do when you get knocked down? What does God want you to do?
3. What has been the biggest thing you have learned from the hard things in your life?
4. What application of the truths of this chapter do you want to make in your life?

---

[1] http://www.landofbasketball.com/records/60_or_more_points.htm

[2] http://www.basketball-reference.com/boxscores/199301160CHI.html

[3] http://www.brainyquote.com/quotes/authors/w/winston_churchill.html

4

I AM NOT WHAT I DO

The Spirit you received does not make you slaves, so that you live in fear again; rather, the Spirit you received brought about your adoption to sonship. And by him we cry, "Abba, Father." The Spirit himself testifies with our spirit that we are God's children.

—ROMANS 8:15-16

For the Spirit God gave us does not make us timid, but gives us power, love and self-control.

—2 TIMOTHY 1:7

OF ALL THE ROOMS IN MY CHILDHOOD HOME, there is one that still holds a special place in my heart. Some of my greatest times of self-awareness came through the deep peace and quiet it offered. The hours of uninterrupted reading gave me insight into the workings of the world. It was a special place where I could be myself without having to rush anything or live up to anyone else's expectations. As I am sure you have guessed by now, this retreat away from the world was none other than our downstairs bathroom. If I close my eyes, I can still see the sink, counter, toilet, little linen closet, and the woodgrain blinds that allowed the gentle sunlight to play across the tiled floor... my own little slice of Heaven!

It was in this secluded retreat where I made one of the greatest discoveries of my life. As I thumbed through the local sports section during one of my regular, Saturday morning visits to the "throne room," some-thing caught my eye: LEAK, RALEY, AND SHUFORD MAKE ALL-STATE. As the reality of the headline sank in, I knew I had to tell some-one. Barely able to contain myself, I screamed, "Dad! Come in here! You've got to see this!" Aware of what my normal bathroom activities included, Dad was reluctant to stick his head in, but after I convinced him it was safe, he opened the door, and we celebrated the fact that I had been named one of the five best linemen in the state. It was a dream come true!

A Season Like None Other

As I drifted off to sleep that night, I replayed the previous football season on the big movie screen in my brain. It had been a heck of a year. Half-way through summer workouts, we had learned that Mom's cancer was terminal, and she had stopped treatments to come home and live out the time she had left with my dad, my brother, and me. Our high school weight room was being renovated, so we had to hold our summer weightlifting sessions outside on the blazing parking lot of the neigh-boring middle school. We were coming off the school's first-ever state championship season and had a big target on our backs every Friday night. We had fought our way through a matchup with a team we had beaten the year before in the playoffs as well as a game against the even-tual Tennessee State Champions who had made the trip south to test their luck against us.

On top of the regular ups and downs of the football season, I had injured my leg in the semifinal playoff game against one of our cross-town rivals. On one of the pass plays during the first half of that fateful playoff game, I cheated a little bit on a protection and got crossed up by the defensive end. Instinctively, I stuck out my leg and managed to trip him up with a (slightly illegal) leg whip. I went back to the line relieved, but it was hard to ignore the throbbing in my lower left leg. At halftime, our trainer, Ms. Perdue, wrapped me up, and I was able to play the rest of the game. We won handily, improved our record to 15-0, and stamped our ticket to our second consecutive state championship game.

However, once the thrill of victory wore off, I was left to deal with the fact that my leg just wasn't right. My dad encouraged me to go to the doctor, and the training staff did their best to get me ready to play. The coaches rode me hard, convinced it was only a deep bruise and that I needed to suck it up. I was absolutely committed to playing in that game. After all, this was the state championship game, and every day seemed to cement the reality that this would be the last football game my mom would get to watch me play on this side of Heaven. So the choice was obvious.

Sitting in the UNC-Chapel Hill fieldhouse before the game, I knew it was going to be a long shot. I had felt the bones popping against each other during Thursday's practice, and simply walking had become difficult. Again, Ms. Perdue worked her magic, and I was feeling a little better about my chances as I walked through the tunnel toward the field. As the adrenaline of the moment captured me, I couldn't resist breaking into my pre-game, lineman jog as I made my way to the spot on the field where I would warm up. About ten yards into my jog, I felt the bones shift in my leg again, and the excruciating pain returned. As any good football player would do, I did my best to mask the pain as I readied myself to play. All I remember about the first couple of series is how incredibly hard it was to drive block, pass block, run… or really do *anything* with my injured leg. I was pretty useless on the field, but there was no way I was taking myself out of a game this big.

The "fatal blow" came after a failed fourth-down conversion late in the first quarter. As I labored off the field, the extra weight I had been putting on my right leg to compensate for my left, suddenly caused me to roll my right ankle worse than I ever had or ever have since. I could feel the shoe on my right foot getting tight as my ankle swelled far beyond its normal size. With a possibly broken leg and a horribly sprained ankle, I knew I was done. But I also knew they were literally going to have to take me out of the game to get me off the field. There was no way I was going to tap out. I still don't know how it happened. I don't know if he saw me hobbling on the sidelines or if it was the merciful intervention of God, but Coach Brown pulled me the next series. My junior football season was over.

The Moment of Truth

We drove straight to the emergency room the next day as we pulled back into town. Having been walking on my leg for nearly a week and a half at that point, I rejected the wheelchair they offered to me and settled into the exam room. As I waited for the results of my x-rays, my head was spinning. *What if my leg isn't broken? What if it was just a bruise and I had quit the last football game Mom would ever see? What if I really was "soft" as the coaches had been suggesting all week? If my leg isn't broken, I'm going to have to find a way to break it myself. There's no way I can face my mom, my coaches, my teammates, or myself if it was a simple bruise.* Sitting here today in my right mind, I can see what an unreasonable train of thought I was riding on. But in the moment, my whole identity seemed to rest on the results of that x-ray.

After what seemed like an eternity, the doctor finally arrived with the manila folder containing the results that would determine my fate. The drumroll played loudly in my head as he pulled the image from the folder and clipped it to the viewer on the wall. As he spoke, I strained to listen, "You must be a pretty resilient young man, walking around here on a *broken leg*." That was it! It was broken! I was vindicated, and the mental picture I had of myself jumped from sissy, weakling quitter to strong, tough warrior who played close to four quarters of football (and a week of practice) on a broken leg. I displayed the boot and crutches around school as a badge of honor. In what seemed to be the greatest compliment of all time, at the end of our celebratory pep rally on the high school football field, our head coach came up to me and said, "Shuford, I'm glad your leg was actually broken." While far from a real compliment, it was light years better than the verbal mistreatment he had ceaselessly heaped on me that season.

It sure felt good to know that, as long as I had my crutches and boot, I was free to revel in my newfound identity "state champion, super-warrior, tough guy"—that is, until the next time when I would have to climb into the ring to earn my identity.

I wish my junior season had been a wakeup call. I wish I had been able to put all the pieces together and see that there was more to life than the crazy game I was playing. I wish I had realized that my identity and my value didn't need to be (and couldn't be) secured by my performance in the game of life. I wish…

Oh, well. Wishful thinking can't change the past, but it can give us a lens through which to view our present circumstances. So, as I sit here, I can't help but follow the rabbit trail of my life's experiences to try to gain perspective on how to move forward in freedom. How did I get to where I was, and how can I keep from going back there? Let's see…

Where It All Began

"What are you doing over there, Scott? This is baseball practice… not a ballet performance!" Coach yelled loudly enough to make sure I heard him from his box behind third base. Unfortunately, with me playing first base at the time, everyone else heard him, too. And like any good six-year-old boy would do, they whipped their heads and eyes in my direction to see what all the fuss was about.

Growing up, I was often the biggest kid on my rec-league teams. I was always number 13 because, as the jersey number went up, the size of the shirt increased with it. I remember thinking that I could easily fit the shirts of the guys who wore numbers 1-4 inside of my jersey at the same time! I don't know if it was because I had grown so quickly or if I was just destined to be a ballerina, but as a boy, I developed a very awkward but comfortable way to stand. I would cross my left leg over my right, put my left heel up next to my right foot, and point my left toes out at a 90-degree angle. It was far from the athletic stance that my coach wanted me in at first base, but it was my go-to move for staying upright when my legs were tired.

So, as what seemed like 3,000 sets of eyes stared at me across the baseball diamond, I became painfully aware of how I probably looked with my legs crossed. As the horror of what they had to be thinking about me filled my mind, I uncrossed my legs, took my best stance at the base, pulled down my cap to block out their burning gaze, and made a mental note that went something like this:

It only takes about 2.5 seconds for your actions to define you as "Ballerina Boy," so be very careful never to do anything that will ever give anyone any reason to think less of you.

While I am not advocating for a new legs-crossed baseball defensive position, I am saying that the way that my coach chose to deliver those remarks opened the door to the road of finding my identity and self-worth in what I did or didn't do.

From there, like some sort of reverse highlight reel, I have flashbulb memories from my journey deeper into the prison of a performance-based identity. Competition seemed only to fuel the fire. Everything I did with my younger brother Zac was a competition. We would play game after game, and once those were done, we would make up new games. We had mudball fights, we would race headfirst down the stairs in sleeping bags, and we played so much NFL Blitz on the Nintendo-64 that we had each other's playbook memorized. Every time, however, I wasn't able to stop until I was the winner. The most upset I remember being was when Zac would beat me in something and then refuse a re-match, leaving me to be the family loser until the next arena of competition became available. It was miserable. I couldn't stand not having an opportunity to prove myself by making up for the sub-par performance I had just put in against my *little* brother. Zac and I are still working through the scars of having a relationship that was largely based on always trying to one-up the other person.

A Tragic Performance

Not only did I look to competition to validate me off the field, the opportunities abounded on the field as well. Between youth league baseball, basketball, and soccer, I was faced with the near-daily pressure to perform. As we explored in the chapter dealing with the joy of sports, the burden to prove myself with every shot, save, or hit began to steal the wonder and excitement of play and replace it with fear and dread.

What if I screw up? What will that say about me? What will *they* think about me?

Without a doubt, middle school was the lowest point in my quest to build my identity. I don't know how to put this politely, but in middle school, I was the fat kid. (Sorry, little Scotty.) During my sixth-grade year, I was beginning to blossom into my offensive lineman body, but the only problem with that was none of the girls I wanted so desperately to impress were looking for a plus-sized guy whose only discernable athletic ability was pushing other people around.

Because things didn't seem to be going so well in this newly discovered arena of competition, I had to find other ways to perform so I could crowd out the "fat kid" part of my identity. True to form, I dove headfirst into working hard to make good grades, earn class-clown status by humiliating myself, and getting after it on the athletic field. My plan almost worked… until seventh grade when I was ineligible to play football because of missing too many days of school, when I got cut from the baseball team, and when the hottest girl in the school made fun of me as I danced around her at our homecoming dance. My whole world seemed to be crashing in. Everywhere I looked, my efforts were coming up short and were only helping to build an identity that I wanted so badly to escape from. How bad did it get? I vividly remember sitting in my room with the lights off, crying my eyes out as I sobbed every word to *Boyz II Men's* "End of the Road." Such dark, sad, and difficult times. All I wanted was to be loved… to have someone tell me I measured up and that I was valuable.

As the journey continued and I began to focus the majority of my efforts on the football field, not only did I *play* the sport of football, I now *was* a football player. As my life became more and more intertwined with the sport I played, it became harder to separate my value and my identity from what I did or didn't do on the gridiron.

This way of thinking started to make its way into other areas of my life as well. From second grade onward, as I tested into "gifted" classes, school performance and grades became other little merit badges I could pin on my coat. And far from freeing me, the successes I had on the field and in the classroom only raised the bar, making it twice as hard to maintain the level of achievement I had already obtained. There was no space to let up because one slip up would define me as a failure, a has-been, and a fraud. I had to keep it up, but that's what being a champion is all about, right? At least, that's what all of my coaches had been telling me.

Most of us would admit we have found ourselves trapped behind the bars of a performance-based identity at some point. Whether we want to admit it or not, we have all asked questions like these: "Did I do enough?" "Do I measure up?" "How does this failure make me look?" "Am I worth it?" The good news for us is that God has dealt with all these questions. We just have to stop performing and believe His answers.

How much are you worth?

What value would you put on *your* life? What about the most valuable player in the NBA? What about the homeless man who lives downtown under the bridge? The richest, most powerful leader in the world? The child in Africa who just lost his parents to civil war? The most hardened criminal behind bars? The most violent terrorist in the world? How much is one life worth?

I vividly remember the summer I spent pricing and cataloguing my baseball card collection. I'll never forget the hours I invested in those little cardboard rectangles, looking each one up in the book, writing the price on a little sticker, and sorting them by value. The whole system was captivating for a bunch of reasons, but the one that has stuck with me the most was the objectivity of the process. An *objective* process is one that is "not influenced by personal feelings, interpretations, or prejudice; based on facts; unbiased."[1] If it had been up to me, I would have given the greatest value to my Jose Canseco and Fred McGriff cards. Why? Because I once saw Jose hit a walk-off homerun at a AAA game in Charlotte, and Fred McGriff had the sweetest mustache of all time! That's why! But thankfully for me, the value of the cards had already been determined. All I had to do was look in the book.

The same is true for every human being on planet Earth. Our value is not up for debate. It is not affected by our actions, nor is it "influenced by personal feelings, interpretations, or prejudices." It has already been determined. All we have to do is look in the book, the Bible.

> Then God said, "Let us make mankind in our image, in our likeness, so that they may rule over the fish in the sea and the birds in the sky, over the livestock and all the wild animals, and over all the creatures that move along the ground." So God created mankind in his own image, in the image of God he created them; male and female he created them. (Genesis 1:26-27)

> Those who trust in their wealth and boast in the multitude of their riches, none of them can by any means redeem his brother, nor give to God a ransom for him—for the redemption of their souls is costly. (Psalm 49:7-8)

> For God so loved the world that he gave his one and only Son, that whoever believes in him shall not perish but have eternal life. For God did not send his Son into the world to condemn the world, but to save the world through him. (John 3:16-17)

> My dear children, I write this to you so that you will not sin. But if anybody does sin, we have an advocate with the Father—Jesus Christ, the Righteous One. He is the propitiation (complete and satisfactory payment) for our sins, and not only for ours but also for the sins of the whole world. (1 John 2:1-2)

> The Son of Man did not come to be served, but to serve, and to give his life as a ransom for many. (Mark 10:45)

THE ETERNAL COMPETITOR

You are not your own; you were bought at a price.
(1 Corinthians 6:19-20)

According to the Bible, our value as humans sounds a little something like this…

We were each intentionally and lovingly created in the very image of God. We were designed to live in a beautiful love relationship with our Creator and to rule alongside of Him here on planet Earth. Our willful rebellion and sin separated us from our gracious Creator and locked us up in slavery to sin and death. Because of His amazing love for His children and because no amount of money would be enough to buy our incredibly precious souls back out of slavery, God sent Jesus, His only Son, to pay the debt we owed. The price for our freedom was incredibly high. The only way that sinful humanity could be purchased was through the shedding of Jesus' blood on the cross. He willingly paid this price by surrendering Himself to death. Because of His sacrifice, our ransom has been completely and satisfactorily paid.

But this doesn't just apply to the best and brightest, the cleanest and nicest, or even to those who say they believe in Jesus. This value has been assigned to every single person on planet Earth! We have *all* had the price paid for our ransom, regardless of what we have done, are doing, or will do. Because this is true, our lives have an unbelievably high intrinsic value that can never depreciate.

You are valuable. Your life matters. Long before you were even born, the God of the Universe looked at you and said, "I want you, and I am willing to pay whatever it costs to have you… even if it means I have to give my own life." There is nothing you did to earn this value, and there is nothing you can ever do to ever lose it. Win, lose, or draw, you are incredibly valuable to your Heavenly Father… no walk-off home runs or mustaches required!

A Cacophony of Voices

"Shuford, you suck!"
"Your teammates have selected you to be a team captain."

"You're the dumbest smart guy I know."

"You are a great leader and a hard worker."

"You only have two speeds: slow and slower."

My performance in sports and competition has been trying to define me for most of my life. It seems like, every time I ask the question, "Who am I?", the words of my coach and my experiences on the ball field jump to the front of the line of available answers. From the highest of highs to the lowest of lows, there is no shortage of experiences to pull from, and that's where the problem lies.

What voice do I believe?

Do I listen to the demoralizing yell from the sideline or the hearty "atta boy" after a game-winning touchdown drive?

What experience do I take as the ultimate one to define my identity?

Is it the crushing block on the screen play to set up the touchdown? Or is it the mental error on third and long that cost us the drive?

Do you see the dilemma? If we are forced to choose from the piles and piles of often conflicting voices and experiences, I am fearful that we will decide solely based on the emotions of a given day. Worse yet, we may be so overwhelmed by the number of options and the gravity of the question that we will let someone else choose for us. Neither of these options will bring about the life and freedom that God has designed for us. They will either cause us to be tossed back and forth like a rowboat in a hurricane or to spend our whole lives living in the shadow of others while trying to fit into the identity that has been forced upon us.

If the words of others and even our own life experiences are not sufficient to form our identity, there must be another source for the answer. Let's see what's behind door number three!

Playing in Slavery

What makes determining our identity so difficult and confusing is that words and experiences really are the basis of finding the true answer. The problem is that, too often, we are listening to the wrong words and examining the wrong experiences. *God's* words and *Jesus'* experiences here on Earth are the only things that have the power to cut through the noise and help us discover our true identity.

As strange as it sounds, I am convinced that I spent the majority of my athletic career as a slave...

A slave to success.

A slave to my coaches' opinions of me.

A slave to my performance and my playing time.

A slave to the fear of failure.

The more I learn about the gospel and the glorious freedom Jesus bought for us on the cross, the more I see what could have been if I had given Him my performance-based identity and allowed Him to replace it with my true identity in Christ. God has so much more in store for His children than living as slaves to the endless quest of trying to "do" well enough to make everyone like them. He desires for us to rest in His love for us and to live and compete with a freedom that allows us to become everything He has created us to be.

Freedom in Action

Ingle Martin was a teammate of mine at Furman, I briefly mentioned him few chapters back, but I think his story is worth diving into in greater detail. He was the stud transfer quarterback from the University of Florida, and I was the red-shirt sophomore left tackle charged with protecting his blindside. We had the opportunity to do some incredible things together on the football field during that season, but what was probably our most impactful moment took place two years ago in the parking lot of a local grocery store. As I sat in my car and reconnected with my teammate on the phone, God used Ingle to paint another beautiful picture of how He longs for us to live and compete as His children.

God really got a hold of Ingle's life during his time in the NFL. Teammates and team Bible studies opened his eyes to the fact that his value, worth, and identity were not based on his performance on the field but rather on Christ's performance on the cross. The gospel changed him. It set him free, and it launched him on a mission to set others free. And that is exactly what he did.

After his time playing professional football, Ingle took over as the head football coach at a high school in his hometown of Nashville, Tennessee. He inherited a program that had gone 5-6 the year before and was in need of an overhaul. Ingle said that the boys on the team were struggling. Their morale was low, their effort was low, and their performance on the field was even lower. He said that everyone walked around on eggshells, afraid to fail. Instead of being arenas in which to strive, to strain, to stretch, and to succeed, the weight room and practice field had instead become places to shrink, to give up, to play it safe, and to fear failure. It was obvious that something was missing, and because of his experience with the freedom of the gospel in the league, Ingle knew exactly what it was.

As he built his coaching staff, Ingle stressed one thing: as a coach, your primary job is to love these boys. He even hired a tight end who had never coached football before because of his unique ability to connect with the players. Even though he was hired to "coach football," Ingle wanted to make absolutely sure that the young men he had been entrusted with had the opportunity to compete in the freedom Jesus offered so they might become everything God intended for them to be.

Ingle told me that, as the new culture of unconditionally loving and valuing each player began to take root, he started to see changes. Once the boys realized that their value wasn't linked to their performance and that there was nothing they could do to make Coach love them any more or any less, they started to bloom. Like tiny oak tree saplings that had finally been allowed to see the sun, they began to lift their eyes to the heavens and stand up straight and tall. No longer were they like hollow shells that labored through every drill with a fearful expectation of punishment. They had transformed into vibrant young men who knew they were loved, and this knowledge brought freedom.

Probably the most profound thing Ingle said to me that day was that his players had been given the freedom to fail. When I asked him what he meant, he said,

> Scott, for years, these boys have heard that they aren't good enough, that they don't have what it takes, and that their

crummy record is a reflection of them as people. They have been so terrified to make a mistake that it has forced them to play it safe for fear of punishment or further consequences. Now that the boys are starting to see that their value lies in who they are, not in what they do, we are starting to see them step out more and go for things they never would have gone after before. They are trying to gain that extra yard or make that impossible interception because they are no longer scared of what will happen if they miss it. Because their identity is secure and they know that we love them unconditionally, they are free to fail... and it is amazing to watch!

While the true victories had already been won in the hearts of each of the young men on the team, further victories followed on the field. That same group of boys who had gone 5-6 the year before burst onto the field the following year with a new freedom and focus. As they took everything that God had given to them and poured it out in the arena of competition as unconditionally loved free men, the results were staggering. Ingle's team went 12-2 and lost in the semifinals of the state playoffs. Since taking over the program in 2011, Ingle's boys have gone 67-6, won one state championship, and haven't failed to make it to the semifinals or beyond each year.

We have been through a lot in our journey of exposing the performance-based identity for the trap it is. I pray that the truth of who you are, because of what Jesus did for you on the cross, is demolishing the lies that the world and our bitter enemy Satan have tried to sell you. You are precious and priceless. God believes you were worth dying for. To live or compete, if even for one second, under any other reality is to settle for less than God's best for you. Does that mean you will win the state championship? Not necessarily. But it does mean you will be free!

__TRAINING TIME__

1. Has there ever been a time where you let your performance (good or bad) define you? Do you still feel that way about yourself and that situation today?
2. What is the danger of a performance-based identity? Why does our Heavenly Father want to free us from such a destructive reality?
3. How would your life be different if you really believed and lived like Jesus had already established your true value? How would it change the lives of those around you?
4. What application of the truths of this chapter do you want to make in your life?

---

[1] Dictionary.com definition

5

BRIDGING THE GREAT DIVIDE

It is for freedom that Christ has set us free. Stand firm, then, and do not let yourselves be burdened again by a yoke of slavery.

—Galatians 5:1

He has saved us and called us to a holy life—not because of anything we have done but because of his own purpose and grace. This grace was given us in Christ Jesus before the beginning of time.

—2 Timothy 1:9

I CAN REMEMBER my first day of college like it was yesterday. My parents followed me down the interstate on the two-hour journey from our home in Charlotte to the campus of Furman University. As we pulled in the front gate, the reality of this new season of life began to set in. Here I was on a campus of a school that just 18 months ago I didn't even know existed, in a city I had never visited, and in a state I often poked fun at when I was growing up. However, all of this was just part of the adventure of being a college student... not to mention a college athlete.

We started at the football offices and then followed the signs to my dorm building, Blackwell Hall. As we pulled onto the lawn outside the front door, I was greeted by the sight of dozens of my teammates unloading everything they would need for the next nine months. There were box fans, computers, couches, and TVs. Each item reminded me that I "wasn't in Kansas anymore" and that the days of living in my parents' "bed and breakfast" (with the occasional yard work!) were over. It was a new day!

It wasn't long before I spotted my roommate, John, and his parents. Honestly, it was hard to miss him! At six feet and six inches tall and weighing close to 300 pounds, he was a mountain of a man. After re-introducing ourselves, we grabbed what we could carry and made our way inside the building. As we searched for our new home, my anticipation grew. I had dreamed about what my dorm room was going to look like... a spacious man cave with posters on the wall, a killer entertainment center, and a little space to do homework between eating and playing video games. As I slipped the key into the lock, my roomie and I braced ourselves for the moment we had been waiting for. Nothing could have prepared us for what we saw when the door opened.

As soon as the lights flickered on, John and I realized there must have been some kind of mistake. We matched our keys with the number on the wall outside of the door and wondered who was playing a joke on us. The rooms in Blackwell were unique to Furman's campus... very unique! Along the right-hand wall were two built-in desks, a built-in dresser, and a small ledge for a TV. The left-hand wall was made up of two three-foot-wide "closets" covered by shower curtains and a set of metal bunkbeds that were built into the wall. The floor space was just barely bigger than a Volkswagen Beetle and was covered in ancient, brown tile. The only redeeming factors were that there was a full-sized window and a mini-fridge with a built-in microwave.

As I wondered how two offensive linemen where going to manage to live in a broom closet for the next year, John laid claim to the top bunk, a decision that would provide much comic relief and many opportunities to grow in faith over the next year! Try laying on the bottom of 40-year-old bunk beds while a 300-pounder does a high jumper's flop onto the top bunk, and you will know exactly what I mean!

That night after we crammed all our things into our tiny room, our parents had kissed us goodbye, and we had eaten dinner, I laid in the bed and stared at the bunk above me with my thoughts going 100 miles an hour. How did I get here? What is life as a college football player going to be like? Who am I *really* going to be?

They say that you have a lot of opportunities to discover who you are in prison… or, at least, that's what I've heard! While I've never been a resident in a prison, I have been a participant in pre-season football camp. The similarities are striking: cafeteria food for every meal of every day, distinctive uniforms, long days working in the sun, a big roommate, no-nonsense prison guards (coaches), and no hope of escape. When you throw in the fact that our dorm room was literally smaller than the average prison cell in the State of South Carolina, the metaphor is complete! Little did I know that my life would be so dramatically altered while "doing time" at football camp my freshman year.

The Wrong Side of the Tracks

When I think back on my childhood years, the image of three train tracks comes to mind. The tracks are running next to each other and heading in the same direction, but they never cross. Due to the way they are positioned, they are just far enough apart that you cannot be on more than one track at a time. It is a picture of a segmented, divided life that I now know is unsustainable, a reality that is made even more evident by the fact that one set of tracks heads slightly uphill, one set takes a gentle downward slope, and the third stays rigidly straight between the two.

Allow me to explain more.

As far back as I can remember, our family has always been in church. We would pray before meals, talk about Jesus at Christmas, and read stories from the Bible. I knew there was a God who had the whole world in His hands, loved the little children, and had prepared an awesome place with streets of gold and angel wings for us when we died. I wanted to make Him smile and enjoyed singing to Him and serving Him at church and in the various ways our parents would lead us to. It was a happy place to be, and it gave me great purpose and peace.

This was Track One, the one with the gentle rise heavenward.

Track Two burst into my life when I was six years old. I was down the street playing at my friend's house when he brought out a magazine he had found in his dad's closet. I didn't have any clue what I was looking at. All I knew was that seeing the naked women on the pages made me feel good. Because the magazine had been hidden by his dad, I made the connection that this was something to be done in secret. I liked the way it made me feel so much that I decided this was something I wanted to do as often as possible. My friend and I spent many of our playdates saturating our minds and hearts with the images on the pages of these newly discovered treasures.

Before long, I decided I wanted to have one of my own. An older boy around the corner sold me one of his magazines, and I finally had the ability to jump on the pleasure train and ride Track Two whenever I wanted. All I had to do was close my bedroom door. No one had ever warned me about Track Two. It started innocently enough, but little did I know, it was silently carrying me downhill.

Track Three is littered with soccer cleats, basketball shoes, baseball gloves, and football pads. You've probably guessed it by now, but Track Three was my sports life. As I mentioned in the previous chapters, I loved this part of my life. It gave me an outlet to compete, to better myself, to spend time with friends, and most of all… to have fun! I loved every minute of my time as an athlete. Some of my most vivid memories from my childhood center around athletic practices, games, or simply backyard play sessions. Through the early years, Track Three was an incredible source of joy and freedom for me. I found great pleasure in pushing the train to see how fast it could really go. Unlike the first two tracks, this one took me neither up nor down, but it served as a steady constant throughout my story.

A Divided Life

Can you see the picture now?

I hope that the three tracks are as vivid in your mind as they are in mine. What you probably can't see as clearly are the well-worn paths in the middle of the different tracks, the places where the grass has been beaten down by the frequent journey between my three different lives. The juggling act was no small feat. On Sunday mornings and Sunday evenings, we would drive 30 minutes south to our church. Every weekday, we would drive 40 minutes north to school and the accompanying athletic practices. Once the other two obligations were complete, I would lock my door and sneak to Track Two for a trip to pleasure town. That was my life, sprinting between three parallel train tracks that never crossed and, in my mind, didn't have anything to do with each other. Track One was to be celebrated, Track Three was to be enjoyed, and Track Two was to be hidden at all costs.

As I got older, the stakes got higher.

Now, not only was I going to church, I was a leader in our youth group. The things of God—worshiping Him and reading His Word—became more and more appealing to me. I had learned to love God truly and to enjoy pursuing Him, and I even felt Him beginning to show me how He wanted to use me to tell the world about Him.

After my mom passed away, I can vividly remember God using me in an unbelievable way to comfort a group of Mom's friends through a Sunday morning Bible study. It was crazy, but the spiritual life of Track One was becoming more and more real to me with each passing day.

Unfortunately, the upward rise of the spiritual side of my life was not enough to keep me from constantly and consistently sneaking back to the selfish, sinful lifestyle that Track Two offered. What started off as an innocent search for pleasure had spiraled into a full-fledged addiction to the images, the feelings they produced, and everything that went along with them. The occasional adventures on Track Two had now become everyday necessities. I would literally plan my schedule around when I was going to be able to take my daily, sinful joyride. The deeper I went, the more I began to realize I was no longer driving the train; I was merely a prisoner onboard.

It wasn't long before my personal struggles began to cross over into my relationship with my high-school girlfriend. In a matter of months, both she and I were chained together onboard this train, barreling into the deep darkness of my sexual sin.

I don't know how to describe to you the feeling of being trapped in and addicted to a lifestyle that you hate. Not only did I hate it, it was killing me. Not only was it killing me, it was destroying my relationships with the people I loved the most. It was destroying everything, and I didn't see any way to slow the train down… much less, get off it.

As I was doing the impossible task of trying to bridge Track One and Track Two, they were moving farther and farther apart. Meanwhile, my athletics life on Track Three flourished. As high school continued, I began to focus more and more of my energy and time on the game of football. I had *played* sports throughout my whole life, but now, I had *become* a football player… and a pretty good one at that (at least, that's what they say!). I found myself being a leader on the offensive line, a three-year starter on the field, and a two-time all-state award winner at the end of my high school career. Our varsity team had gone 47-1, and I had three state championship rings to show for it. But as I shared before, thanks to a verbally and emotionally abusive coach and a hyper-competitive and extremely transactional culture, I began to lose the joy, freedom, and pleasure that had once made this train ride so appealing. As I steamed forward on an almost-inescapable collision course with college athletics, I often wondered exactly what was just over the next hill and if I would even like what I found.

You may remember that, in the movie *Mrs. Doubtfire*, Robin Williams disguises himself as an elderly English nanny to have the opportunity to sneak around his ex-wife and spend time with his kids. It is hilarious! While watching him transition between the gruff television actor and the prim-and-proper housekeeper with a British accent is entertaining, from the viewer's seat, most of our laughs come at his expense. In one scene, his rubber mask falls out of the window and gets run over by a truck, forcing him to cover his face with a whipped cream "facial" to avoid being discovered. In probably the most painful (and hilarious!) scene of the movie, Robin Williams is torn between two dinner dates at the same restaurant… one with the "real" him and one with "Mrs. Doubtfire." As he jumps between the two tables, changing his costume in the bathroom in between personas, all the drama and comedy that you would expect to come with trying to live two lives in one space comes out. It's a mess!

Just like Robin Williams, my life was divided. It was hopelessly split between not just two but three different realities that could not exist in the same space. To make things worse, I felt like I was having to run faster and faster between the tracks to keep up with the trains. Sadly, for me, this was not a feel-good movie with a happy ending. This was my life… and it was confusing, depressing, and downright exhausting.

Let's call a timeout.

Spotlight

Let's take the spotlight off me and point it at you… at your heart. I want to see if any of this resonates with you and your own story. Do you feel like your life is compartmentalized in any way? Do you feel like there are places to be lifted up, places to be embraced and enjoyed, and places filled with so much shame and guilt that they need to be locked away so no one will ever find out about them? Are there any areas in your life that require you to put on a rubber mask and take up a new accent to not be found out? Have you ever wondered why the spiritual side of your life had to be locked in its own little Sunday morning world, unable to touch any other part of your existence? Do ever get tired of running back and forth between the tracks? Do you ever look for a way out?

I sure was tired. I was looking for a way out. Little did I know, the way out was also looking for me.

Derailed

Fast-forward to my time in prison—I mean… freshman football camp! I had come to campus as the same worn down and divided young man who had finished his high school football career six months earlier, but I was hopeful that the change of scenery would help me. After all, I had met some neat players and coaches during my recruiting visit who seemed like they might be able to help me on my journey. As the recruiting process came to a head, I had felt God leading me to choose Furman for that very reason, and I was excited to see what the new season held.

About a week into camp, almost miraculously, my high school girlfriend of three years called out of the blue and said she thought we needed to take some time apart. I didn't fully understand, but as I tried to wrap my mind around why she needed to step back, I felt God urging me to seek Him on the matter. I had prayed about things before, but this time, it felt different. It felt like my seat on the spiritual train on Track One was my true home. I spent hours with God, talking, listening, and asking Him for His direction. It was during this season when my spiritual life was on high alert, my world of sexual sin had been put on pause, and I was all alone to make my own decisions in the "real world."

I had known about Jesus and had even trusted Him as my Savior, but I didn't have an intimate relationship with Him. I had sung a thousand songs and done a hundred things for Him, but I had never seen His face. I had read His Words over and over again, but I had never heard His voice. All that changed during the fall of 2003.

One day, while I was spending time with God in my dorm room— I got what I like to call my "knock at the door." While I didn't hear an actual knocking on our metal door, I *knew* at that very moment God was pounding on the front door of my heart. The choice to open the door seemed simple, and as I did, I saw Jesus down on one knee, holding out a wedding ring with a simple request: "Will you marry me?" Now, I didn't actually *see* Jesus, but the image is so clear in my heart that I could still paint a picture of the scene today. It was totally unexpected and completely overwhelming.

In shock, my first thought went to how messed up and broken my life was. I was far from sinless and even farther from the person I would imagine Jesus would want to marry. I mean, that's a lifelong and, in this case, eternity-long commitment on His part. I couldn't fathom why He would want *me*. I told Him how I wasn't perfect and that I would probably only end up breaking His heart, but it didn't seem to faze Him. It was like He knew everything about my past, present, and future, yet He still wanted me anyway.

I then began to wonder what it would cost me if I said "yes." Would I have to quit football, drop out of school, and follow Him to the mission field in Africa? Was He going to call me to get rid of the things that brought me fulfillment before I could follow Him? How different would my life look? Maybe this would be a good thing. But then again, is He sure He wants all the baggage that comes with me?

Even though my head was spinning, I knew what the answer had to be.

My relationship with God had been like a motorboat floating down a river with the engine off. I was drifting in the right direction and bouncing off the occasional rock or stump, but I wasn't heading on any particular path with any particular purpose. I was tired of my halfhearted approach to life, and I was *really* tired of the three-track shuffle that was slowly killing me. There had to be a way out of the madness. So with as much faith and conviction as I could muster, I looked Jesus in the eyes and said "yes."

Now, before I lose you or you get too hung up on the imagery of Jesus wanting to *marry* you (I'm an old married guy, so it makes sense to me!), let me give you some pictures from the Bible that show God's heart and desire to choose you and to be your *everything*.

He Wants YOU

In the first three pages of the Bible, God created man. Until this point, God had created everything by simply speaking it into existence and calling it "good." But when it came time to create humankind, the pinnacle of His brilliance, God stooped down and took up a handful of dust. Once He had formed it into the perfect shape, He breathed His own breath into our nostrils and called us *very good*. The Bible says that, once He created our earliest ancestors, He literally walked and talked with them in their garden home. It was clear from day one that He wanted to be their God and wanted them to be His people.

As the story moves on, God's people had wavered in their faithfulness to Him, but his devotion to His most beloved creations never changed. As He was leading His people out of Egypt after the more than 400 years they spent there among the many temples and false gods, God made a stop at a mountain called Sinai. You may have heard them called the "Ten Commandments." But if we look closer, they could also be viewed as an adoption ceremony. In them, we see a Father's heart for

His children as He teaches them a new way of relating to Him and to the world—as His beloved, chosen children.

While I have never adopted a child, I have several close friends who have. The process illustrates God's heart in an unbelievably beautiful way. From their stories, I gather that it goes something like this:

- A child is born into a situation that is neither healthy nor beneficial for his or her survival or long-term growth.
- The child is given up for adoption with the hope that someone will provide a better future for him or her.
- The parents seeking to adopt are presented with a potential child.
- After much prayer and wrestling with the decision, they choose whether to adopt the child.
- If they choose to adopt the child, he or she goes home with them and becomes a true part of their family.
- The child is chosen.
- The child has a home and a new last name.
- The child is loved.

This is exactly what God wanted to happen on Mount Sinai. He *chose* His people and called them by name. His intention was clear: He wanted to be *their* God, and He wanted *them* to be His people.

He says it this way in the book of *Exodus*:

You yourselves have seen what I did in Egypt, and how I carried you on eagles' wings and brought you to myself. Now if you obey me fully and keep my covenant, then out of all the nations you will be my treasured possession. Although the whole earth is mine, you will be for me a kingdom of priests and a holy nation (Exodus 19:4-6).

He called His people to put away all other false gods and idols and to love and worship Him only. He also called them to leave their selfish, sinful ways behind and to honor Him by loving each other.

> I want to be your Father, and I want you to be My child. Will you leave your old way of life behind, learn My new way of living, and let Me take you as My own?

When God extended the offer of adoption to His people, He wasn't offering them an equal partnership in the relationship. He wasn't saying, "My house is empty without you, and I need you to complete me." Rather, He was saying,

> I am the God of the Universe who made you and everything you see around you, and I want to offer you the opportunity to come into My home and join My family. But make no mistake… I AM GOD.

The reason I know this is true is because, when speaking of this exchange on Mount Sinai, the Bible says,

> When the people saw the thunder and lightning and heard the trumpet and saw the mountain in smoke, they trembled with fear. They stayed at a distance and said to Moses, "Speak to us yourself and we will listen. But do not have God speak to us or we will die." (Exodus 20:18-19)

We can't reduce God to a cosmic buddy. He is God, and the fact that He wants an intimate relationship with us is both awe-inspiring and humbling.

However, despite their fear and uncertainty, God's people accepted His offer, packed up their bags and moved into His house. Even though God was unwavering in His faithfulness to care for His children, we have continued to wander back to our old lifestyle – choosing the "pleas-ures" and "freedoms" of life on the street over the warmth and security of life in His home.

Some years later, due to His precious children's continued drifting and enslavement to sin, God sent Jesus to open the path to complete adoption once and for all. The Bible says it was God's great love for the world and His intense longing for every single one of us to walk in rela-tionship with Him that led Him to pursue His wayward kids at the ex-pense of His Son's life (John 3:16; 1 Timothy 2:4). His commitment to us while we have been and continue to be uncommitted to Him is truly unfathomable.

The Bible puts it this way:

> On the day you were born, no one cared about you. Your umbilical cord was not cut, and you were never washed, rubbed with salt, and wrapped in cloth. No one had the slightest interest in you; no one pitied you or cared for you. On the day you were born, you were unwanted, dumped in a field and left to die. But I came by and saw you there, helplessly kicking about in your own blood. As you lay there, I said, "Live!" And I helped you to thrive like a plant in the field. (Ezekiel 16:4-7)

> Yet to all who did receive him, to those who believed in his name, he gave the right to become children of God— chil-dren born not of natural descent, nor of human decision or a husband's will, but born of God. (John 1:12-13)

> The Spirit you received does not make you slaves, so that you live in fear again; rather, the Spirit you received brought about your adoption to sonship. And by him we cry, "Father." The Holy Spirit himself testifies with our spirit that we are God's children. Now if we are children, then we are heirs—heirs of God and co-heirs with Christ,

if indeed we share in his sufferings in order that we may also share in his glory. (Romans 8:15-17)

Isn't that incredible? Because of what Jesus did to our sins on the cross, God has made a way for us to enter into His family—to be fully adopted as His child forever.

God desires to be our God, but He also longs for a personal, intimate, trusting, lifelong relationship with us. He wants to take us as His child.

A Miracle...

What happened after I opened the door to Jesus was truly a miracle. I don't know how to describe it other than to say that God literally took Track Two out of my life. I had been fighting it as hard as I could. I had even been reading *Every Young Man's Battle*, an incredible resource in the arena of masculine sexual purity. But when I said "yes" to Jesus, something unexplainable happened. It was as if He had taken 20 tons of dynamite and blown closed the mouth of the tunnel leading down to the train of sexual sin. I looked the next day, and I could find no traces of my former enslavement. He had completely and utterly removed pornography and everything that accompanied it from my life. As I sit here writing this today, I am 14 years free from the obsession that had seduced me from the age of six. Gone is the addiction. Gone is the darkness. Gone is the shame. The light has come. Praise God!

While I know that this is not everyone's story, and while I acknowledge that this complete and instant 180-degree turn was an incredible miracle from God, I just have to share what He did for me. I spent too long believing the lie that I was doomed to a lifetime of bitter struggle and repeated failure and defeat. I can't shout it loud enough, that whatever your struggle is—addiction, self-image, eating disorder, rage, hopelessness—Jesus is *alive*, and He is willing and able to set you completely free.

Not only did Track Two cease to exist—and I cannot describe to you what a miracle that was!—but the spiritual life of Track One and my athletics life of Track Three started to merge, an experience that started my life as an athlete moving on an upward trajectory and shook the last area of compartmentalized division out of my life. My friend Chris Shepherd says, "When you open the door to Jesus, he doesn't just want to rearrange the furniture; He wants to blow up the house!" And that is exactly what He did! He changed everything, and my life has never been the same.

God created you and me to live in relationship with Him in such a way that *every* part of us is in alignment with that relationship. As a baseball bat is operating in its intended purpose when it is hitting a baseball, we are walking in our intended purpose and design when we are living in the freedom and wholeness that Jesus offers.

__TRAINING TIME__

1. What are the different "tracks" that your life has been divided between? Are you tired of the juggling act yet?
2. How does knowing that Jesus wants to marry you and give you the gift of an undivided life make you feel? Have you said "yes" to His proposal, or are you not yet ready?
3. Try to describe what living an undivided, free life would look like for you.
4. What application of the truths of this chapter do you want to make in your life?

6

TRUE TEAMMATES

And let us consider how we may spur one another on toward love and good deeds, not giving up meeting together, as some are in the habit of doing, but encouraging one another.

—HEBREWS 10:24-25

Therefore confess your sins to each other and pray for each other so that you may be healed.

—JAMES 5:16

WITH MY OVERWHELMING STRUGGLE with sexual sin out of the picture and with football and my faith moving on the same track, my life took on a whole new direction. If middle school and high school had been like living in a dark cave, college was like being on the most incredible playground you could imagine in the middle of the most beautifully sunny day ever. It sounds like an over statement, but everything came easily, everything made sense, and I couldn't have been more free.

In high school, my teammates had been buddies, but the bulk of our relationship had been confined to the weight room, practice field, and stadium on Friday nights. I love my high school teammates, but looking back, I longed for us to be so much more than lifting partners and pass blockers. I truly wanted for us to be brothers... to laugh together, to cry together, to fight for one another, to know God better, to walk in victory over sin, to encourage one another, to give our all in *every* arena of life, and to make each other better.

I think that is what we are created for. No person is meant to be an island out at sea by themselves. Jesus sent His followers out in pairs of two. The early Church leader Paul always had someone with him. In one of my favorite pictures of how we are supposed to move together, the Bible says,

> And let us consider how we may spur one another on toward love and good deeds, not giving up meeting together, as some are in the habit of doing, but encouraging one another—and all the more as you see the Day approaching. (Hebrews 10:24-25)

This thing called following Jesus is designed to be a team game, and just like in any team sport, you need teammates.

A Whole New World

In a world where hundreds of teens join gangs every year, where you can buy more "friends" on social media for the right price, and where depression and suicide rates are climbing, a true team can be the family that so many people are looking for. You compete together during the season, sweat and bleed together in the weight room, spend countless hours together in meetings and travelling to away games, and in some cases, even live together with your teammates. You will be in each other's weddings, hold each other's children, and revel together in stories of the "good old days" at reunions. You will be the first to know about a sickness, divorce, or death in the lives of your teammates, and you will be the one most strategically positioned to say and do just the right thing at just the right time to breathe life and hope into the situation. God made something special when He created the concept of "team," and I believe that He has placed you *exactly* where you are and has surrounded you with the teammates He has for a divine purpose. You can be more than *just* workout partners. You can be TRUE teammates. You just have to run after it!

I didn't realize it when it was happening, but my time as a football player at Furman changed my life. As I became more and more comfortable and confident in my newfound, one-track life, I began to embrace the reality that God really had called me to play college football, that His Kingdom extended even to the farthest reaches of my sports life, and that my coaches and teammates were gifts straight from Him. When I lay my experiences over the framework of how the Bible urges us to live as members on Team Jesus Christ, some neat things jump out. Let's take a look!

Choose Love

> A new commandment I give to you, that you love one another, even as I have loved you, that you also love one another. (John 13:34)

Eleven times the New Testament, we are commanded to "love one another." This love is fleshed out further in Paul's letter to the Corinthian Church where he says,

> Love is patient, love is kind. It does not envy, it does not boast, it is not proud. It does not dishonor others, it is not self-seeking, it is not easily angered, it keeps no record of wrongs. Love does not delight in evil but rejoices with the truth. It always protects, always trusts, always hopes, always perseveres. Love never fails. (1 Corinthians 13:4-8)

This is what a TRUE teammate looks like, and I can't fully describe for you the transformative impact that this kind of love can make on team. John writes,

> No one has ever seen God; but if we love one another, God lives in us and his love is made complete in us. (1 John 4:12)

In a sense, we show the world what God looks like when we love each other!

During the four and a half years I spent as a TRUE teammate on a real team in college, I had countless opportunities to love and be loved by my brothers on the gridiron. As we each individually fell in love with Jesus, we couldn't help but shower that same love on each other. Through encouraging text messages and conversations throughout the day, late-night spiritual conversations at Waffle House, and visiting each other's families on the weekends and breaks, we laid our lives down for each other as Jesus Himself modeled. The most transformative force at work during my experience as a college football player was the love of Christ being poured into my life through my teammates who were themselves being filled by the same love.

Built for Tough Times

> Bear one another's burdens, and thereby fulfill the law of Christ. (Galatians 6:2)

A burden can also be called a heaviness, weight, or trouble. And if you are a part of a team or family, you are sure to encounter one if not several of these during your journey together. I need both hands and both feet to count the significant deaths and family tragedies that have impacted my teammates both while we were playing together and during the years since we have gone our separate ways. As we have heard Jesus promise to us before, "In this life you will have trouble." Brokenness abounds, and it seems that the deeper you journey with someone, the more it will come to the surface. I am glad that Jesus follows that statement up with the encouragement that we can "take heart" because He has overcome the world (John 16:33). The crazy thing is that He often chooses to make this vital truth evident through *us*.

During the 2005 pre-season camp—not even a week into our grueling, two-a-day practices—one of our teammates got a call that his father had taken his own life. The sudden loss hit all of us hard, and nearly the entire team made the two-hour road trip to stand in solidarity with our brother… to bear his burden with him.

In 2010, one of my former teammates lost both his grandfather and his father in in a span of two days. Several of us made the journey to North Carolina to help bear the moment with his family, and I have done my best to continue to encourage him as he continues to love and support his mother through her grief.

I will never forget what it meant to me to have my high school teammates surround our family at my mom's funeral.

There is something so beautiful and redemptive when family members (and a real team is a true family) hold each other during times of heaviness, weight, or trouble. This is what Jesus had in mind when He taught His disciples to care for each other. This is a mark of a TRUE teammate.

It's Not About You

> Do nothing from selfish ambition or vain conceit, but with humility of mind regard one another as more important than yourselves. (Philippians 2:3)

Jesus left *everything* He had in Heaven and humbly became a human just like us. Because of His great love for all of humanity, Jesus was compelled to lower Himself and to lift us up. In the truest sense of the word, He regarded *us* as more important than Himself, a reality that was made evident by His actions.

When I imagine this concept with flesh on it, I can't help but think about Brandon Berry. Brandon came to Furman as a 180-pound wide receiver and finished his career as a 223-pound fullback. That's just the type of guy he was. He cared more about the team and everyone on the team than he did about himself. He not only demonstrated this by adding more than 40 pounds of bulk to his 5-11 frame, but he also was the FCA President on campus, regularly got up early on Sunday mornings to gather guys and take them to church, spearheaded a team Bible study complete with a (somewhat illegal) bonfire, and led a gospel singing group of football players affectionately referred to as "The Shower Boys." During our two years together, Brandon invested literally hundreds of hours into my life, and I am forever indebted to him and several other teammates who took the time to put selfish ambition and vain conceit aside to serve those around them humbly.

Lift Your Voices

> Let the word of Christ richly dwell within you, with all wisdom teaching and admonishing one another with psalms and hymns and spiritual songs, singing with thankfulness in your hearts to God. (Colossians 3:16)

As strange as it sounds, God's desire is for His Word to impact *every* part of your life. Not only does He want to rearrange your life through His Word, He wants you to use His Word to sharpen the other Jesus followers in your circle. In the verse above, it seems like Paul is saying that, as God's Word takes up residence inside of us, we will not be able to keep it from spilling out of us in the form of teaching, encouraging, correcting, and *thankful singing*!

While there were numerous times that my brothers on the team used God's Word to shape me for the better, some of my sweetest memories come from the team shower room. It was there that a group of 8-12 of us would take Paul's advice and sing psalms, hymns, and spiritual songs to God with thankful hearts. The thankfulness usually stemmed from a big victory on the field or the end of a particularly difficult practice, but we would usually use any excuse to break out in song. We would sing old gospel songs at the tops of our lungs for what seemed like an eternity, and between the hot water and the bathroom acoustics, we sounded like a Heavenly choir! Although it's hard to explain to "outsiders," when I reflect on some of the best times with my brothers in Christ on the football team, these shower-choir times rank high on the list!

Lean on Each Other

> Therefore, confess your sins to one another, and pray for
> one another so that you may be healed. (James 5:16)

Like the persistent beep of an alarm clock, the Bible is unwavering in its insistence that our faith journey is not meant to be travelled alone. This thing called following Jesus has been and will always be a team game. It's just too difficult. There are things that are just too heavy to carry alone. We have too many blind spots. We are not strong enough.

On a Thursday night after team Bible study, one of our younger teammates came up to my buddy Austin and me with tears in his eyes. He looked completely broken and as if he had been running gassers all day long. After we all sat down, he confessed that he had screwed up and that his girlfriend was pregnant. He was extremely upset with himself and about the situation, but it was his confession that allowed the freedom of Christ to take control of the situation. As he laid his junk out on the table, God's Holy Spirit brought some words from the prayer that King David had written after he came to grips with his sin.

> For I know my transgressions,
>   and my sin is ever before me.
> Against you, you only, have I sinned
>   and done what is evil in your sight...
> Purge me with hyssop, and I shall be clean;
>   wash me, and I shall be whiter than snow...
> Create in me a clean heart, O God,
>   and renew a right spirit within me...
> Cast me not away from your presence,
>   and take not your Holy Spirit from me.
> Restore to me the joy of your salvation,
>   and uphold me with a willing spirit. (Psalm 51)

As God's Word did the work that it promises to do in situations like that, and as we prayed for our broken brother, it was so evident that what was happening in that offensive line meeting room was something so much bigger and deeper than anything that the simple game of football could offer. This was true, spiritual brotherhood.

Run the Race TOGETHER

> And let us consider how we may spur one another on toward love and good deeds, not giving up meeting together, as some are in the habit of doing, but encouraging one another. (Hebrews 10:24-25)

As I mentioned earlier, the passage above is one of my favorite sections of Scripture that deals with the beauty of running the faith race together with spiritual teammates. As a matter of fact, I have built much of my understanding of ministry and the Church around the principles it highlights. I especially love the simple, cut-and-paste application that it holds for us in the athletic arena. There are three things that the author of *Hebrews* commands us to pursue with each other: 1) spurring one another on toward love and good deeds, 2) meeting together, and 3) encouraging one another. If you take these concepts at face value, they are incredibly powerful. But if you dig a little bit deeper, they shine even brighter.

"Spur one another on toward love and good deeds…"

What do you do with a spur… especially if you are a cowboy? I've seen enough cowboy movies to know that spurs are meant to be kicked into the horse's ribs to urge him to go faster. And that is exactly what the author of *Hebrews* is suggesting we do to each other! In the original Greek language, the word we translate as "spur" meant to irritate or to provoke. How about that! We are all used to being "spurred on" in the weight room or on the court, but what about in the spiritual arena? Are we willing to give *and* receive a kick in the ribs in order to run faster toward "love and good deeds"?

"Meeting together..."

Every team game has a huddle. Whether it is a quick gathering during a stoppage of play or a pre-play circling up to receive the play and snap count, these times are vital to the team moving forward *together*. My supervisor Tim Steele pointed out that a huddle exists for three reasons: *encouragement, accountability,* and *direction*. I have found this to be true throughout the entirety of my athletic career, whether it was a hearty "great block!" or a pointed "pick it up!", the huddle was invaluable.

The same holds true as a member of Team Jesus. We *must* have times where we "huddle up" with other believers for encouragement, accountability, and direction. But we must be careful not to get a delay-of-game penalty by staying huddled together too long. We must huddle, but we must run the plays, too!

"Encouraging one another..."

I will never forget when Debo "encouraged" me during my freshman year. We were doing off-season conditioning, and I was still trying to find my stride as a college athlete. As we rounded the corner of the field on the third of what seemed like one million laps, I was already breathing heavily... very heavily! You could say I was exerting maximum effort... or so I thought.

Being two years older and wiser than me, Debo grabbed me by the sleeve and yanked me over next to him. In his gruff voice, he barked, "Quit breathing like that!" He then demonstrated how to slow my breathing down and actually use the oxygen I was sucking in and blowing out. He stayed beside me until I caught the rhythm. Then, he motored away. I had just been "encouraged" by a 290-pound grizzly bear!

Again, that is exactly what the writer of *Hebrews* had in mind! The word he used in the original language literally means "to call alongside." It is the picture of two friends running as the one in front looks back to urge the other to catch up with him. It is a simple but profound "Let's Go! You can do this! Come on up here!" This is something we all need so desperately as we run the long, challenging race Jesus has marked out before us.

Once you are free and whole in Christ, you are not left all alone on a desert island. You have been drafted onto the greatest team of all time: Team Jesus! Whether you are currently part of an athletic team, a business team, or a family team, God desires to infiltrate that world and turn your siblings, business partners, and workout partners into powerful spiritual teammates.

Will you answer the call?

___TRAINING TIME___

1. Do you think that our relationship with God is an individual sport or a team game? Why?
2. How has your life been impacted by a TRUE teammate? How have you been a TRUE teammate to someone else?
3. Who do you "meet together" regularly with? Who "spurs" you on to love and good deeds? Who are you "spurring"?
4. What application of the truths of this chapter do you want to make in your life?

7

THE LIGHTBULB

...those who hope in the LORD will renew their strength.
They will soar on wings like eagles; they will run and not
grow weary, they will walk and not be faint.

—ISAIAH 40:31

I pray that the eyes of your heart may be enlightened in order
that you may know the hope to which he has called you, the
riches of his glorious inheritance in his holy people, and his
incomparably great power for us who believe.

—EPHESIANS 1:18-19

I SHOULD HAVE SEEN IT COMING. The look in our offensive line coach's eyes gave it away. He was in love. The object of his love? Six-foot-seven, 261-pound high school senior Joel Bell.

Joel's parents had been missionaries in Egypt and Croatia during Joel's childhood, and his only exposure to the game of football had come through grainy VHS tapes of old Dallas Cowboys games. Joel had always loved the game but didn't have an opportunity to step onto an American football field until he was in the eleventh grade. As a somewhat gangly and often distractible newcomer to the game, Joel went largely unnoticed by many colleges... that is, until my coach laid eyes on him.

The way that Coach talked about him made him seem almost too good to be true: a huge frame to bulk up through Furman's weightlifting program, a raw athleticism to be harnessed and refined, and as a relative infant in the game—no bad habits to break. We could tell that Coach had found a project that he was sure would pan out in the long run. He had surely uncovered a diamond in the rough! We all knew that Joel was going to be something special.

When Joel joined the team, I was fresh off my redshirt year and was playing backup left tackle behind senior Ben Bainbridge. Ben was a great example for me to learn from. He was a quiet, hardworking guy who finished as an All-American. I enjoyed having some space to learn the game and pick up the pace of college play, but I was also excited about the prospect of starting at left tackle the following year and being able to contribute to the team.

As a career offensive lineman, I am forever indebted to the number of football movies that give faces, names, and value to the "big uglies" up front. Thanks to several on-screen dynamos like big Louie Lastik from *Remember the Titans*, the general public can see that us big guys have hearts, feelings, and in some cases… even a little soul! Having played left tackle for the majority of my football career, I am particularly enamored with a movie that came out in 2009 called *The Blind Side*.

My Position

The movie begins with a woman's voice speaking while a clip from the 1985 Monday Night Football match-up between the Washington Redskins and the New York Giants plays in the background. She breaks the play down frame by frame with a keen eye on Joe Theismann, the quarterback, and Lawrence Taylor, the opposing defensive end. The play is a flea-flicker where the running back tosses the ball back to the quarterback to throw downfield. But, in this case, the defensive line isn't fooled. As Theismann steps up to throw, he is crushed from behind by a charging Taylor. Instantly, Taylor jumps to his feet, wildly motions to the Redskins' sidelines, and then grabs his head with both hands as if he had just accidently done something terrible. Joe Theismann's right leg was shattered, his shin bone had broken through his skin, and his sock was filling with blood, he would never play another down of football.

As tragic as this freak injury was, this was the moment—at least, according to the woman's voice—that changed football forever. Coaches were forced to realize that a quarterback could avoid the rushers he *could* see but was much more susceptible to those he *couldn't* see... those who were coming from his "blind side." The game has adapted accordingly as, now, left tackles are some of the highest paid players on several of the NFL teams across the country. If there is a "most valuable" position on the offensive line, it is the left tackle—at least, that's what the sports writers and fans think! As a continued boost to the ego of us blindside protectors, the narrator continues with her praise of the position:

> The ideal left tackle is big, but a lot of people are big. He is wide in the butt and massive in the thighs. He has long arms, giant hands and feet as quick as a hiccup.[1]

So that's who I had been for four years, 47 wins, and three state championships in high school. That is who I had been for thousands of plays in practice and roughly a hundred plays on Saturdays during my first two years at Furman.

But when I saw the way Coach looked at Joel Bell, I began to wonder if my days as the "anchor" of the offensive line were numbered. Even so, I wanted to be the man, so I pushed and worked as hard as I could to be ready for my moment on the big stage.

Is it all over?

The 2005 season was one that will go down in the record books. Literally. As I am writing this, the 2005 Furman team still holds the record for the most powerful offense in the history of the program. We averaged 470 yards per game, 6.2 yards per play, and our quarterback, University of Florida transfer Ingle Martin, had 3,123 yards passing. We engineered several last-second comebacks and were ranked as the number-one team in the country at one point during the season. We made it to the final four in the NCAA FCS (then Division 1-AA) playoffs and lost to the eventual national champs by only six points on a fluky goal-line stand. Talk about an incredible year! Oh, and I almost forgot to mention… Guess who played all 1,061 plays at left tackle? Yours truly!

As we made the long bus ride back home from our season-ending playoff loss, my mind was flooded with thousands of different emotions. I was saddened by the fact that our storybook season had ended the way it had. I had wanted so badly to have the honor to play for the National Championship. I was upset by the goalpost-tearing, bus-rocking, profanity-laced antics of the other team's fans after the game. I was grateful to God for the opportunity I had been given to play such an important role on such a special team. I was excited and overwhelmed by the likelihood that I, Scott Shuford, could actually be a three-year starter on the O-line.

However, as soon as I let my mind wander and begin to imagine the accolades my future had in store, I was reminded of my now 6'-8", 308-pound teammate named Joel who, after two years in the system, was guaranteed to have a starting spot on the line the following year. This thought made me anxious, and the internal dialogue began…

What if he takes my spot?

I'm sure they are going to put him at left tackle. I mean, look at him! He is a thousand times more athletic than I am. They aren't going to sit him to the side while I do the most important job on the line.

If he takes my position, where will I go? I don't remember how to play any of the other positions. I am a left tackle.

Will I ever start again?

Will I ever even play again?

Should I just quit now?

I know what you're thinking… "Relax, Dude! You just finished one of the most incredible seasons of your life. Drink it in. Celebrate a little bit. Don't worry about next year. God has it all under control."

I know! I know! Even though I had surrendered my life to God and had given Him full control of everything, I still struggled to shake the "what ifs" that haunted me on that bus ride home. I knew He was in control, but what if I didn't like the way He painted out my next two years? What if my plan and His plan were different? What then?

Somehow, I managed to drift off to sleep that night, and although the fear and anxiety weren't completely gone in the morning, they had been overshadowed by a drive and desire to embrace head on whatever God for me. Bring it on! Let's go!

The Big Switch

As I had imagined, Coach informed me that Joel would be playing left tackle in the upcoming season and that I would have a chance to compete for the left guard spot. Humbled but not discouraged, I handed my position to my much larger and more athletic brother and began to prepare myself to make the transition from tackle to guard. Again, I can imagine what you "non-linemen" are thinking: "Isn't every offensive line position the same? Don't they all just grunt, sweat, and push on other guys? They're pretty interchangeable, right?"

Well, after I take a second to cool off from your incredibly offensive and uninformed assumptions, I will attempt to answer those questions. Just give me a minute. Us linemen are a quiet but proud bunch.

Okay... I'm better now. Let's see... What did you ask? Are all the positions the same? Not at all!

Using a war-time analogy—which you have to do when you are playing football—the picture looks a little something like this. The tackles are like the fighter jets. They are out in space, doing their best to counter the moves of a faster, more-athletic defensive end. Sometimes, a win for them is to get the opponent simply to "fly by" the quarterback and take himself out of the play.

The guards are the tanks. They are in the trenches doing hand-to-hand combat with defensive lineman who play the role of and bear a physical resemblance to a wrecking ball. The guard must build a wall, and giving up three inches is three inches too much!

The center is the general in the command center. They make the calls that direct the rest of the line. His job mostly consists of helping one of the guards in his task of stopping and pushing back the human bowling balls lined up across from them.

"Don't they just grunt and sweat and push on other guys?" I am going to pretend I didn't hear that question and move on.

"They're pretty interchangeable right?" Sometimes, this actually is the case. I know some offensive line coaches who rotate all their guys through the different positions to try to find the best match up. This requires a lineman who is just as good at going right as he is left, who can easily switch in his mind the side of leverage he is able to allow, and who can remember *and* execute all the tackle, guard, and center plays from *both* sides of the line.

There are some who excel at being this type of "renaissance man" offensive lineman. But for me, it was a struggle. I had no problem learning the guard plays, but the leverage and different types of things I was being asked to do with my body were difficult to say the least.

With all that being said, I actually had a very productive spring playing guard next to Joel and was excited about the prospects of the upcoming year. It had been 11 years since I had suited up at guard, but I was ready for the challenge!

Game Time!

My junior year was an interesting one on and off the field. The previous spring, I had been selected to replace my good friend Nick Sanders as President of Furman's FCA Chapter, an exciting but slightly overwhelming opportunity. My girlfriend (and future wife!) Jess had just graduated, packed up, and moved three and a half hours away to Charleston for nursing school. And I had gotten somewhat passed over in the roommate shuffle and was living with three very different guys who I wasn't particularly close to and in a building I had never been in. All of this was happening while I was trying to master the art of being a tank. (Oh, yeah... And I was going to class as well!) My life was full to say the least!

The 2006 football season stated off with a bang! We won our first two games and took ACC contender University of North Carolina down to the wire, losing a 45-42 heartbreaker as they scored on their last possession. I was doing okay in my new position. It was still a big adjustment, and I blew some plays against the monsters on UNC's D-line that still haunt me today, but I thought I was doing as well as could be expected... or, at least, as well as our other guard.

Our next game, a home matchup against conference foe Western Carolina, was a physical beat down. We only ran 48 offensive plays, but we gave the ball to our fullback, future NFL Pro-Bowler Jerome Felton, on 20 of those plays, and he scored six touchdowns, a Furman and Southern Conference single-game record that still stands today. I can vividly remember several plays where I thought to myself, "I'm getting the hang of this guard thing!" It was an awesome, physical victory.

We beat Wofford by two touchdowns the following week to set up a showdown with Coastal Carolina the next Saturday. As we pulled onto the campus in Conway, South Carolina, I was the starting left guard on the number-three team in the country and was ready for the fight. Coastal had only started football three years earlier and was still looking for their program's first marquee win over a bigtime program. We were convinced it wasn't going to happen on our watch!

The game was a close one. Our two running backs combined for 230 yards on the ground, and their future NFL wideout Jerome Simpson went off for 151 yards on nine catches. Talk about a prize fight! It was back and forth for three and a half quarters until Coastal pulled ahead by two with five minutes left in the game. We mounted two game-winning drives that ended in a failed fourth-down conversion and a sack that forced a fumble. As time expired, we sat on the wrong end of a two-point deficit, and Coastal Carolina celebrated its program's first big win. Needless to say, there was a lot to think about on the five-hour bus ride home.

Turning Point

I can remember exactly where I was sitting when Coach gave me the news.

"Scott, I'm the coach, and I have to make these kinds of decisions. It's just not working out with you at guard. We are going to go with Andrew and move you to backup tackle behind Joel."

As soon as he said, "It's not working out," it felt like time stopped, and everything I had ever done on the football field came rushing into my mind. I remembered my first football helmet and the pee-wee game we had played in the freezing rain. I remembered the time I accidently caught the ball while playing center at practice in middle school and when I rode the bus to our first away game. I remembered the feeling in the weight room when our first state championship rings arrived and how much pride I took in wearing my varsity letter jacket during the winter months. I remembered passing the conditioning test during football camp my freshman year and what a joy it was to be a part of a brotherhood on our college campus. I remembered the 1,061 plays I had started at left tackle the year before and how close we had come to going to the national championship.

But none of that seemed to matter anymore. It all seemed to hinge on this moment. Once Coach finished his sentence, two options ran through my mind:

One, I could have jumped up, started yelling, flipped Coach's desk over, and made the case for why I was at least as good as the other guard. Defend yourself! Fight for what is rightfully yours!

Two, I could accept what Coach was saying, step back to process what it meant, and trust God with the next steps.

As my mind raced and as I estimated whether or not I could get the desk completely over, I truly felt that I heard God's voice inside of me, saying, "Scott, this is a part of your story." His voice cut through the noise like a knife, and I knew I could trust Him. I thanked Coach for everything he had done for me, assured him I would do everything I could to play my role on the team, and made my way out of the football building to clear my head.

Benched

If you have lived long enough, I am sure you have been there. It's that place where your reality doesn't match your expectations, where your visions don't come to life, and where your dreams die. It is a terrible, gut-wrenching place to be, especially when you have poured so much of your sweat and blood into something, only to have someone tell you it's not working out... that you aren't good enough. When that happens, we all have a choice to make. Will you fold, or will you have faith? Will you explode and grasp for control, or will you choose peace and give God control? What will you do?

For me, the question had already been answered in the fall of my freshman year. Jesus had offered to take me as His own, and I had surrendered. My life was now His. He had earned that right by what He had done on the cross and by what He had done to demolish the track of sexual sin and merge the tracks of football and faith. He was driving the train now... not me. If I was really going to journey together with Him, I was going to have to trust Him. Even when it didn't make sense...*especially* when it didn't make sense. He had shown Himself to be good, to be in control, and to have my best interest in mind. What did I have to fear?

Despite that my life—my past, present, and future—was secured squarely in the hands of the God of the Universe, the next game was tough. It was a major struggle to watch the sport I loved and the teammates I cared so deeply about seemingly pass me by. It felt like my heart had been removed from my chest and that I was frozen in ice where I was able to see and hear what was going on around me but was unable to affect anything that was happening.

I vividly remember my first game on the bench. I had started every game of my varsity career in high school, I had played every snap of the previous year's playoff run, and I hadn't left the field this year. Yet, here I was on the sideline. My role had now been defined as "backup tackle," behind All-Conference senior John Kivett and the eventual All-World man-child named Joel Bell. With the next game going right down to the wire, I didn't see any action. Not one play.

After I finished the usual postgame drill of smiling for pictures on the field with my family, I turned to walk back to the locker room. My head was spinning as I walked, and the questions that had jumped me in Coach's office once again pestered me like a cloud of mosquitos.

What just happened?

How did I end up here?

What did I do wrong, and what can I do to get back on the field?

I've worked so hard. This isn't fair.

Should I just quit now and save myself further embarrassment?

I changed quickly, not even needing a shower, and made my way up the steps to face my friends, family, and the questions I didn't know how to answer. I knew that, if I didn't find them soon, the season and much of what God had been building into me would be lost.

What *Really* Counts

I think we are all tempted to believe that the only reason to join a team or participate in sports is to get playing time and that, if you aren't contributing on the field, you aren't glorifying God, and you aren't valuable to the team. Ultimately, we believe it's all about *me*. Where does the truth really lie?

When we trust Jesus' payment for our sins and surrender our lives to follow the one true King, He makes good on His most amazing promise literally to move into the neighborhood and set up residence *inside* of us. Jesus made this promise to us:

> ...the Helper, the Holy Spirit, whom the Father will send
> in my name, he will teach you all things and bring to your
> remembrance all that I have said to you. (John 14:26)

If that was not the case, I don't know where I would be today.

As I laid in bed that night, the Holy Spirit took me to school. My mind and heart were flooded with hope and peace, and the questions that had appeared so overwhelming just hours before now seemed like faint shadows in the light of the truth. All I could hear was God's voice reminding me that He loved me, that He was in control, that I was His son, that this was a part of my testimony, and that He still wanted to do a great work through me at Furman and on the team. With the sweet words of the Heavenly Father who had walked me through the turmoil of secret sin, the drama of middle school, the death of my mother, and the abuse of high school wrapped around me like a blanket, I drifted off to sleep knowing that tomorrow would be a new day.

The rest of my junior year felt like a science experiment. God was the scientist, I was the rat, and the football field and college campus were the laboratories. It seemed like I was turning new corners and running into exciting new realities every day. As I put more and more of what I had learned into practice, I became undeniably convinced that, in my life as a college football player, there truly was more available and more at stake than I had ever realized.

As a member of a football team, I had always gauged my contribution by what I was able to offer between the lines on game day. Sure, I could be the first one in line for drills at practice and help out the younger guys on the team, but my *real* impact was measured in minutes played, sacks allowed, and pancakes. (In football, a *pancake* is when an offensive lineman manhandles his opponent.) My on-the-field performance told me whether or not I was doing a good job and affirmed all of the hours of work I had invested in the offseason.

The Good Doctor

In His infinite wisdom and love, God knows *exactly* what we need, and He is able to deliver right on time, every time! I thought I had been seeing clearly, but my lenses needed to be adjusted. It looked as though God had scheduled me for an appointment with the Divine Eye Doctor.

I don't know about you, but I hate going to the eye doctor! I have always been on the (very!) sight-challenged end of the spectrum, making it a difficult and stressful process. They always seem to take me through the same drill. First, they take me back to the exam room and have me remove my contacts. Once they are out, I am literally blind! In one recent trip, an assistant who was unfamiliar with my predicament tried to get me to read the eye chart without my trusty contacts. It was all I could do to squint out the giant "E" at the top of the poster!

After the initial exam, I usually follow the sound of someone's voice as they lead me to another tiny room to undergo a few more very-difficult-while-blind tests before returning to the exam room to wait in hazy darkness for the doctor to arrive. When he enters the room, I do my best to shake his hand and engage in small talk while he sets up the refractor, the big machine with a bunch of lenses and dials on it. Once he places his magical machine over my eyes and I commit myself to looking through it, everything changes. The fuzzy blobs on the wall in front of me take on the familiar shapes of the letters I have read my entire life. Definition and clarity replace the foggy uncertainty of my first few minutes in the office.

Usually, I am content to be able to read the larger letters on the chart because, after all, it's so much better than it was when I was blind. My doctor, however, is not as easily impressed. Just as I am about to thank him for making it "good enough," he begins to twist and tweak the gears and lenses of the refractor like a mad scientist. "Is it better here? Or here?" "This one? Or this one?" "Is it clearer here? Or here?" Try as I might, even after a lifetime of eye doctor visits, I still cannot figure out a rhyme or reason to the process or how he knows which direction to turn the knobs. I guess I just have to trust his knowledge of the eye… what it's made up of, how it works, and what needs to be done to make it operate at its highest potential.

I guess God wasn't pleased with me being able to see "well enough." He wasn't going to settle until He got me to 20/20. As He stripped away football—the reality and lens through which I had been viewing the world—I was left blind. I was paralyzed and frustrated by my inability to engage the world in the way I always had. I was reduced to the status of a blind and disabled person whose only hope was to follow the guiding voice and to wait patiently for the Good Doctor to come into the room. It was at this point—when I had been reduced to my bare, naked, insufficient state—that the door opened, the lightbulb came on, and the Doctor went to work. I was living out the reality of Paul's prayer for his friends in the early Church:

I pray that the **eyes of your *heart*** may be enlightened in order that you may know the hope to which he has called you... (Ephesians 1:18)

The challenges and opportunities continued to roll my way as the season progressed, but something was different. Gone was the "poor, pitiful me" attitude that left me paralyzed. I was now filled with a stronger and clearer passion, purpose, and drive than I ever had been before. Paul's prayer had worked. The *eyes of my heart* had been enlightened, and I now knew the hope toward which I was being called.

With my junior season wrapping up, I took my now-clearer focus and locked my eyes on my senior season.

TRAINING TIME

1. Have you ever had a moment when your entire life's story passed before your eyes and you realized that you were standing at a crossroads in your testimony? Describe how that moment impacted your life.
2. Has the Holy Spirit ever given you the gift of seeing the deeper, eternal reality in your competition?
3. Describe how this new perspective has changed the way you live, work, and compete.
4. What application of the truths of this chapter do you want to make in your life?

---

[1] *The Blind Side*

8

VICTORY LAP

And let us not grow weary of doing good, for in due season we will reap, if we do not give up.

—GALATIANS 6:9

You are the light of the world. A city set on a hill cannot be hidden. Nor do people light a lamp and put it under a basket, but on a stand, and it gives light to all in the house. In the same way, let your light shine before others, so that they may see your good works and give glory to your Father who is in heaven.

—MATTHEW 5:14-16

SENIOR YEAR… Wait. Cue the music, and dim the lights. That's more like it. Let's try this again…

Senior year… Here it was, my final season of football. I had been a football player for the past 14 years of my life. Once the season started on September 1, the ride was going to be over in just 77 short days. I knew we were guaranteed to play 11 games in the upcoming year, and I also knew that each game was 60 minutes long. In football time, I only had 660 minutes left to be on the game field with my brothers. Thankfully, due to the work God had done in me over the past season, I also knew I had countless opportunities and moments in the weight room, locker room, and on the practice field to put what I had learned to the test. Bring it on!

Mat Drills

Every athlete says it, but it really is true: there is no offseason. When the final horn sounded, signaling our loss to the Bobcats of Montana State and the end of my junior season, a wave of emotion flooded over me. Perhaps, it was the altitude or the frigid wind ripping through my body, but I sensed a turning of the page. I spent the majority of the plane ride home playing the upcoming season over and over again in my mind. With All-Conference tackle John Kivett graduating, I knew that the right-tackle position would be mine to lose. I made up my mind right then and there that I was going to do everything in my power to fight for that position while not losing the precious gift of vision and focus God had given to me during the past season. As the earth raced past beneath me, I leaned my head against the plane window and finally drifted off to sleep, excited to see what God had in store.

Like the end of every football season, I gave my body a few weeks to recover before the itch started to take over. I'm not talking about poison ivy. I'm talking about the itch to get back in the weight room and back on the field. One of our coaches at Furman always said that, "if you ain't getting better, you're getting worse." After a couple of weeks of eating and sleeping (and classwork, of course!), I knew it was time to start getting better. Our coaches were more than happy to help us in that process by scheduling a delightful little thing called *mat drills*.

Mat drills are simple enough to explain. The whole team, including the coaching staff, piles into the basketball arena for a time of bonding and physical betterment. That physical betterment comes in the form of sprinting drills on the basketball court, agility drills beneath the shoots, weaving through ladders and cones, and of course, the shuffling, rolling, and diving on the old wrestling mats that gave the whole carnival its name. I forgot to tell you that this took place at 5:45 a.m. three times a week during the entire month of February. Oh, and did I mention that the coaches were not exactly thrilled about having to leave their wives and children at home in their warm beds to come "encourage" us through our early-morning routine. As you can imagine, there was always a little edge to the winter festivities on the mats.

My First Rodeo

I will never forget mat drills during my freshman year. I made the mistake of going home the weekend before and had brought some sort of head cold back with me. If I had been bundled up in a recliner next to a warm fire, it wouldn't have been too bad... just some sinus pressure and a stuffed-up nose. But unfortunately for me, I was about to be tossed into a coliseum full of other warriors and lions/coaches who were looking to pounce on any sign of weakness. Sitting in my locker with my head between my knees after the first mat drill, my brain struggled to put complete thoughts together. But when it did, those thoughts sounded like this:

How could 45 minutes last so long?

How could the coaches see everything that everyone did?

I am so glad that guy screwed that rep up and had to go again. I needed the time to catch my breath.

How am I going to make it through this?

I am going to die.

How can I break my leg to get out of this torture?

I was facing a greater level of physical challenge than I ever had before, and it was driving me inward to a place of selfish self-preservation. As a 19-year-old rising sophomore, I had not developed the framework to be able to excel through the trial. At this point, I was merely surviving. Like tax season or an annual eye exam (the horror!), mat drills showed up every year with relentless consistency. There was no escaping the fiery trials of February, so like a captive in a maximum-security prison, I developed a plan to keep my head down and simply survive. Little did I know, God had something He wanted to teach me through the sweat and pain of the mats.

Bringing Purpose to the Mats

Fast-forward to the end of my junior year. The football season was over, the itch was on, and February was quickly approaching.

Over the years, my body had gotten used to the beatings of mat drills, forcing the battle deeper into my mind and soul. Still not content with my "survive at all costs" strategy, my roommate Austin Holmes (a wiry defensive back) and I set out to figure out the point of mat drills. Why did God keep forcing us through the "excitement" of February each year, and what did He have for us to learn through it? Given the new perspective I had on competition, football, and life, I was all ears for how even mat drills could propel me toward my goal of looking and moving more like Jesus.

After praying and wrestling through all of the possible things God was trying to teach us through our time on the mats, Austin and I reached the conclusion that God wanted to draw us outside of ourselves and teach us how to truly love others, even while we ourselves were dying. We decided that we were going to give our very best in every drill and that, instead of being consumed with ourselves, we were going to do everything in our power to encourage our brothers on the team as they fought through their own personal struggle with mat drills. We prayed and asked God for strength and courage. Then, we (strangely enough) eagerly anticipated the first 5:45 a.m. mat drills.

What God did in my heart and life during my final year of mat drills still goes down as one of the most tangible examples of what can happen when we seek Him and fight to engage even the tough places in life, like Jesus would. In seeking to encourage and lift up my brothers on the team, I found my heart and mind being transformed. No longer were my thoughts consumed with "me," "my," or "I." They were now filled with "him," "them," and "they." My plans to escape by breaking my leg and my prayers that others would fail so I could have more rest were replaced with plans to put an arm around a poor freshman while he struggled to breathe. My new aim was to offer prayers for God's strength, joy, and peace to dominate my teammates—and, yes… even my coaches. I had more energy than I ever thought possible when I took my eyes off myself and off the clock. The workouts seemed to fly by. It was awesome!

Miracle on the Mat

One of the outcomes of this renewed mindset was so unexpected and unbelievable that I wouldn't have believed you if you told me beforehand it was going to happen. Each day, at the beginning of our workout, the coaches would award a coveted purple shirt. The purple shirt went to the top performer in each group during the previous day's drills. With the team split up between offense and defense and big/medium/small, there were only six shirts to go around, and the competition was pretty intense. As we sat in our designated square on the basketball court before the second day of mat drills, Coach made his pre-drills remarks and began to hand out the purple shirts. I had never been the most impressive athlete, and because our group contained linemen far quicker and stronger than me (insert Joel Bell), I tuned Coach out and began to set my mind to give all of myself to God and my brothers during the upcoming workout.

When Coach called out my name, it shot me back to reality. "The purple shirt for the offensive bigs goes to Scott Shuford."

What?! Me?! There must be some kind of mistake...

After the look in Coach's eyes assured me that there was no mistake, I jogged up to receive the faded purple t-shirt that served as my prize. The applause of my teammates and the feeling inside of me rivaled any victory I had ever won. I had the purple shirt. God had allowed me to win the purple shirt! I competed, led, and encouraged with all my heart that day, and I was overflowing with joy, humility, and gratitude at the opportunity to lead my team in such a way. While I knew I was training for an audience of One and that I didn't need a purple shirt to affirm my revised mat drills game plan, it was a really neat cherry on top!

As I took my place on the court before the next early-morning workout, I smiled at the recollection of getting to lead the previous drills as the purple shirt. What an honor. As I thought about how much fun it would be to have that opportunity again, my name again shook me from my thoughts. "Purple shirt... Scott Shuford." There was no way. I knew I had to be dreaming now. All I had done the previous workout was try to give my all and to love my brothers. Wow.

This is the part I wouldn't have believed if you had told me, but I went on to earn the purple shirt *every* day of my senior-year mat drills tour. By the end of the month, it became sort of a joke: "And the purple shirt goes to… surprise, surprise… Scott Shuford." But I can assure you I wasn't laughing. With every shirt God allowed me to have, this new way of living that called me to give my all for an audience of One while fighting to love those around me with the love of Christ sank deeper and deeper into the foundation of my soul, and I knew I would never be the same. I was becoming more like Jesus through the love and prayers of a teammate and a crazy thing called mat drills. Who would have imagined it!

During the month of February, we got a new offensive line coach. The coach who had recruited me, built into me, believed in me, and modeled a true teacher-coach was taking a job elsewhere, and we were going to have a new leader. While the news was sad, it didn't affect me too much. I was on a mission that was far greater and was playing for a Coach who was far higher than anyone they could bring in to steer our unit. I lifted my eyes and kept putting one foot in front of the other, determined to make this my best season yet. Little did I know, God had something even greater than a string of purple shirts in store for me.

An Incredible Honor

Reporting to football camp as a freshman, I remember being in awe of the older guys. They were so much bigger, stronger, quicker, and older than I was. I dreamed of the day when I would be in their shoes. Even though all the old guys were impressive, the guys who really stood out were our team captains. They were the superheroes on and off the field. They were the ones who would eventually be All-Americans and who were tasked with leading our team through every phase of the season. During my second year at Furman, linebacker Mike Killian was a team captain. He had a tattoo of the Grim Reaper on his arm, complete with his football number etched on his robe and a 9mm pistol in each hand. Now, *that* was a football team captain!

I had optimistically set some performance goals for myself coming into Furman, but being a team captain had never crossed my mind. That was for someone else. That was for some hotshot quarterback or linebacker, not for a slightly-more-athletic-than-average offensive lineman. Besides, I didn't have the menacing tattoos or killer instinct I had so often seen from that position. And let's not forget the fact that I been benched and spent the last half of my junior season serving Gatorade to the starters on the sidelines. Me? A captain my senior year? No chance. Forget about it.

Well, despite my best arguments about why it would never happen, Coach announced at a team meeting that I had, in fact, been voted a captain by my teammates. Talk about a shock! There was nothing that could have prepared me for the flood of emotions that accompanied my newfound role. On one hand, I was overjoyed and so proud of the honor. On the other hand, I was dumbfounded and confused.

I spent the next couple of weeks arguing with God and trying to convince Him He had made some kind of mistake in allowing me to be named a captain. I tried to remind Him that *real* football team captains were freak athletes who demanded the respect of their teammates. And as a last-ditch effort, I even brought up the fact that I hadn't played a meaningful snap of football in over eight months. I don't think I was scared as much as I was confused and concerned about what kind of captain I could be from the sidelines.

After listening patiently to my incredibly well-thought-through and logical arguments, God quietly said, "Son, listen to me. They *have* captains like the ones you are thinking of. They *need* a captain like you." That pretty much sealed the deal for me. I didn't understand, and I wasn't quite sure how it was going to work out. But all I knew was that my brothers on the team had chosen me to lead them. Not only had God allowed it, He seemed to be endorsing it… so I had better get on the Scott Shuford for captain train!

As I embraced the reality of my position of leadership, my mind raced back to the teammates who had made the greatest impact on my life. There were a handful of guys who were way more than fellow football players. They were TRUE teammates and brothers in the realest sense of the word. I thought of how Brandon Berry had pulled me into his room during my freshman camp and had spent hours asking me questions and pouring into me. I thought also of how he had led a group of us through *Wild at Heart* and how the vulnerability and oneness we experienced around that bonfire never left us. I also remembered how he had woken up early to drive across town with Austin Holmes and me to spend time in prayer and worship before our day started. There were also vivid memories of Danny Marshall's goofiness, Brad Cooper's encouragement, Clayton Dyson's old-man wisdom, Brian Bratton's calm cool collectedness, Patrick Covington's steadfastness on the field, and Corey Stewart's fire. My mind was flooded with examples of guys who had gone above and beyond their role as a football player and had truly embraced the joy of servant leadership. I determined in my heart that I would be a man for others like they had been for me.

The rest of the offseason was a blast! I was a team captain. I was a senior. I was slated to be our starting right tackle. I was healthier, stronger, and bigger than I had ever been. I had my eyes squarely fixed on competing and leading like Jesus. And in the greatest victory of my life, I married my college sweetheart, Jess, on June 23 and stepped into the incredible arena of being a married college student-athlete! It looked like it was shaping up to be one heck of a final season.

The Last Dance

My senior season began with the opening kickoff against Presbyterian College on September 1, 2007. I took the field at right tackle in front of the crowd of 11,000, and we commenced to dominate the Presbyterian team. We won the game by a score of 40-16 and reveled in starting the year off with a big victory. As was customary, once the game got out of hand, we put in the reserves, and my backup Thomas Slaughter (such a perfect football name!) finished the game off on the right side of the line.

Our next game was against Hofstra University in Long Island, New York, a team we had beaten in triple overtime two years before in a slugfest at Furman. We made the long plane flight up the East Coast and piled into the tiniest visitor locker room (if you could call it that...) I had ever seen. It was not my best night. I spent most of the evening trying to catch up to the guy lined up across from me and felt rather poorly about my performance after we lost the game. This was the first real test of my new mindset in competition, and I must admit it was tough. Travelling so far to play such an intense matchup and then to come up short in a way that potentially cost the team the chance to win is a difficult pill to swallow.

It's easy to give God the glory and to play for an audience of One when everything is purple shirts and getting voted captain. It's a little more difficult when you have to ask yourself the tough questions that follow a loss. It was obvious that I had still had work to do physically, mentally, and spiritually to become the competitor and man God wanted me to be.

While we had already been rotating a bit, after the Hofstra game, our new O-line coach let us know that Thomas Slaughter and I would be more intentionally splitting time and that whoever graded out the highest at the end of each game would start the following game at right tackle. Obviously, this was not what I wanted to hear, but I took it as well as I could. Our previous coach had been an all-or-nothing guy who didn't believe in splitting time between players, and I had grown to identify with his philosophy that it was the starter's job to lose. I think that there is something special that you carry into a game when you know you are going to be the man, and I think it is incredibly difficult to bring the same intensity and focus if you are coming off the bench. However, it was clear that my personal preferences didn't matter much at this point. The challenge had been laid down, and I was going to embrace it.

Let's call a timeout.

A Whole New World

I don't know how to tell you what a difference the experiences during my junior season and senior offseason made in my life. I had been stripped down and brought lower than ever through the experience of being benched. Through the darkness, God had shown Himself to be enough for me. He had proven Himself to be the only one who was faithful, loving, and strong enough to walk with me through the process of changing the way I viewed the world. Not only had He done that, He continued to surprise me with the ways He chose to place me in positions of leadership on the team. He was patiently and steadily making me look like His Son Jesus, and it was my job to stay on the exam chair and let Him finish His work. If I quit or lost focus, I would never fully embrace what He was trying to give to me. Boy, it was tough, but I knew it was good. I had come too far and seen too much to turn back.

Time in!

Back to the Dance

The third game of the year was against a little school called Clemson University. With Clemson's campus only being 45 minutes from Furman, I had been down several times to visit buddies who were attending school there, not to mention I had been in the stadium the last time we had played the Tigers during my true freshman year. Aptly named Death Valley, which holds more than 83,000 screaming crazies who are decked out in more orange clothing than you ever thought possible, it is an awesome place to play! Being a captain, I got to be on the field for the coin toss as the Clemson team ran down their famous hill and through an enormous cloud of what had to have been more than 2,000 helium-filled balloons that made their way skyward as the band played.

There is something special about playing the "big schools" that we got to play. It's almost as if there are no expectations and that you are free to give it your all. I can't explain it, but for some reason, I felt the most unrestricted in front of the largest crowds and stiffest competition. Clemson was no different. I played my heart out on every snap that Coach gave me and cheered as loud as I could for Thomas while he did the same. We lost the game, but it was an experience of a lifetime.

On the Monday following the Clemson game, we gathered together as an offensive line unit to review the tape and receive our grades. While I can't remember my exact grade, all I know is that Thomas' was higher, making him the starter for the following week's game against Wofford. When Coach made that announcement, it felt like a big spotlight had been pointed squarely at me... not just in my eyes but at my heart. My mind raced back to the exact spot I was sitting the year before when my previous coach had taken the ball out of my hands. While the reality of the situation was the same - I was no longer a starter on the Furman offensive line. Something was different. Instead of the urge to defend myself or flip some piece of furniture, I was filled with a peace and assurance that the God who walked with me through my junior season and had blessed me in so many unexplainable ways in the offseason and beyond would never leave me. I knew this was a part of His plan. And, besides, I had already learned that my *true* impact on the team came in many other places beyond the game field. I still wondered how a team captain could lead from the bench, but God continued to assure me that He had gotten me into that role and that He was going to be the one to make it work.

One Last Hurdle

Perhaps, this is a testament to the fact that I was still in need of some heart transformation—which I will *always* be in need of this side of Heaven!—but I don't have very many on-the-field memories from the rest of the season. My final eight weeks of football and college are summed up in a handful of flashbulb memories, some high and some low, that are forever ingrained in my soul.

The first memory is one of the most difficult for me to bring up. It is not hard to think about because I am still haunted by it. No, I have made great peace with this part of my life and story and know now that God was firmly in control the whole time. It is difficult to bring to light because I love and respect my senior-year offensive line coach, and the last thing I want to do is to paint him in a bad light. We have a great relationship today, and he still prays for our family and ministry daily. And I truly thank God for crossing our paths. With that being said, I feel like there is no way to separate my experience senior year from the rest of my story. So here is what I remember.

Thomas Slaughter continued to grade out higher than me. He continued to be the starting right tackle, and I continued to be the backup under Coach's plan to allow us to split time. Like I mentioned before, it was tough to bring the same level of mental and spiritual focus to the game as a reserve player. I never knew exactly when I would go into the game or how many plays I would get on a given Saturday, but I tried to remain thankful for *any* opportunity to contribute on the field while I continued to encourage and serve from the sidelines.

As the year went on, I began to notice that I was getting fewer and fewer chances to get in the game. What had begun as a 50/50 or 60/40 split was now an 80/20 divide between the time Coach allowed Thomas to play and the time I was in the game. We continued to compete for the starting spot with the highest scorer getting the nod, but my chances to get on the dance floor seemed to be shrinking by the week.

During one particular game (I honestly cannot remember which one), I played extremely well while Thomas had one of the rougher nights of the year. On Monday, as we took our seats in the film room, I still felt good about my performance and the prospect of getting to take the field with the starters that weekend. My grade sheet reflected my optimism as I had graded out significantly higher than Thomas, but the number of plays I had participated in (18) gave me a reason to hesitate. According to our grading system, you had to be above a certain score after 20 plays to "grade out." Coach didn't mention anything to Thomas or me during the meeting, so I figured I would be the man and went about preparing my heart and mind to start the game on Saturday.

We would go over the finer details of our offensive line game plan and address any last-minute issues during our meeting time together on Thursdays. After Coach wrapped up his teaching points, he listed the starters for the weekend's game. When he got to right tackle, he said that, because I didn't have enough plays to grade out the previous game, he had decided to grade the film from the week's practice sessions instead… and that Thomas was going to be starting on Saturday. I had been in this situation enough times before to anticipate the punch in the gut that those words brought with them, but what I hadn't planned on were the faces of my teammates. As soon as Coach delivered the news, which came as a shock to all of us, 11 heads snapped in my direction, and 22 eyeballs locked on mine, looking to see what my response would be to such an unexpected turn of events. All I can say is that God's Spirit showed up at the very moment I needed Him. I managed to swallow hard and do the first, most Christ-like thing that came to mind: nod and say, "Yes, Sir."

Crossing the Finish Line

I have always said that what the world is searching for is not some form of religion that controls just your Sunday mornings or political thoughts. The world is longing to find something *real*. They are looking with a quiet desperation that they themselves might not even be able to put a finger on for something that will truly carry them when the chips are down and the bottom drops out. The Bible says that, when God is in control here on Earth, the evidence is "not a matter of talk, but of *power*" (1 Corinthians 4:20). In short, when someone's life is wrapped up in God, that person should have to say very little; the power and peace with which they live and move should testify to a lost and broken world that there truly is something greater, stronger, and deeper that will hold them through any storm. While my trials in football were not even worth mentioning in the same breath as the life-and-death struggle my sweet mother faced, it was comforting to know that my trust was planted firmly on the same rock that had sustained her years before. It was on this solid foundation that I finished my football career.

In a way that only He could have pulled off, God made the most of my final lap at Furman. Despite the loss of opportunity on the field, I found myself swimming in chances to use the influence that God had given me as a senior football player and team captain for His glory. There was the incredible team Bible study I had the opportunity to co-lead with some of my dearest brothers on the team. There was the tearful conversation full of hugs, prayer, and Scripture after one of our brothers revealed that his girlfriend was pregnant. There was the opportunity to pour into a lively freshman from Michigan who occupied the locker next to mine. There were the pre-game captains' talks (sermons!) that my position allowed me to deliver to my football family every Saturday. And who could ever forget the spirited gospel songs that echoed through our Friday night team chapel services and rattled the walls of our locker room shower.

My joy had been found. My identity had been set. I was living the dream and walking in everything God had for me. Finally.

My career as a football player came to an end on November 17, 2007 at 3:22 p.m. in Cullowhee, North Carolina. The 52-21 victory reflected the passion and fire that we all played with that day. Every snap was a precious gift, and we 19 seniors knew it. As the clock struck zero and signaled the end of a season and, for many on our team, the end of a nearly lifelong pursuit of the game, I was overcome with a flood gratitude. It was gratitude for the men and brothers who had made my time at Furman so special, gratitude for all the opportunities God had given to me to take my talents and put them in the mix on the football field, and most of all, gratitude for the man I had become through the process.

Did it turn out precisely how I would have painted it? Not exactly. But as I laid with my brothers in the end-zone grass, staring up at the clear, Western North Carolina sky—not wanting to take off my pads because I was sure I would never put them on again—I knew I wouldn't trade it for the world.

___TRAINING TIME___

1. What are your "mat drills"? What is it like to approach those arenas in a worldly and selfish way? What is it like to move in a godly, selfless way?
2. Describe a time when you experienced tangible fruit of competing with a godly perspective. How was it different from other times?
3. Describe a time when you were holding onto a godly mindset, yet things didn't "work out" in the eyes of the world. How did you maintain your focus?

4. What application of the truths of this chapter do you want to make in your life?

9

OPEN YOUR EYES

Do you have eyes but fail to see...?

—MARK 8:18

He took the blind man by the hand and led him outside the village. When he had spit on the man's eyes and put his hands on him, Jesus asked, "Do you see anything?" He looked up and said, "I see people; they look like trees walking around." Once more Jesus put his hands on the man's eyes. Then his eyes were opened, his sight was restored, and he saw everything clearly.

—MARK 8:23-25

AS I REFLECT ON MY TIME AS A COMPETITIVE ATHLETE, I can't help but be swept away by both the beauty and struggle. I am still left in awe by all the life-long relationships and deep lessons learned. It was a glorious time of my life—although, sometimes tragically so—and I will be forever grateful for the greatest present my time on the field gave me: a new perspective. I would like to try to wrap that present back up and re-gift some of the highest and best points to you. However, before you can tear off the shiny bow, I need to ask you to put on a special pair of glasses.

Once you have the glasses in hand, be sure to pay close attention because it would be a shame to finish this book and live the rest of your life missing the depth and richness that our magnificent God has hidden just beneath the surface of our everyday reality.

A New Set of Glasses

I remember vividly the first time I wore 3D glasses. I had a subscription to a little magazine called *Disney Adventures*. Once a year, they would produce a 3D issue that would come complete with a fully functioning pair of 3D glasses. Each year, as I would scour the pages to find the "high-tech" cardboard glasses, I would glance in eager expectation at the content of the magazine. My excitement level was heightened by the fact that I couldn't really tell what was on each page; the jumbled blur of superimposed images and red and blue lines was like a secret treasure map just waiting to be decoded by my superglasses. I couldn't get them on fast enough!

Once I carefully tore along the perforated lines and taped on the ear pieces, the red and blue lenses opened my eyes to the wonder that had been awaiting me! The characters seemed to jump off the pages, and stories I thought I knew took on a whole new life. My reality had been shifted by simply looking at life through a slightly different lens.

As recorded in the Bible, Jesus was constantly trying to get His message across to His followers. Everything He said and did during His ministry on Earth was expertly crafted to open people's eyes to the presence of a deeper reality. When He said that the poor are rich, the last will be first, and the only way to really live is to die, He wasn't merely having a case of "opposite day." He was offering a new set of glasses through which people could view the world. He knew that, if they could begin to see the world like He does, their lives would be transformed.

Let's get back to the pair of glasses in your hand. By now, you have probably been trying to figure out what magical world they are going to allow you to see. You may be excited, or you may just be skeptical. I wish I could personally sit with you and convince you of how deeply important it is that you put the glasses on, but all I can do is write as LOUDLY as I can: PUT THEM ON, IT WILL CHANGE EVERYTHING!!!

Look a little closer.

Okay, now that we are on the same page, let's take a look at them. Hold them up. What do you see? The first thing you probably notice is the thick, sturdy frames. This is a vast improvement over the cardboard and scotch tape that constituted the 3D glasses of my youth. These frames can literally withstand anything. For thousands of years, people have been trying to destroy them by burning, crushing, and burying them. Yet they have survived without a scratch. You won't win any beauty pageants wearing them (think "rec specs"), and your friends may laugh at how you look. But you can be assured that you are joining a long line of champions—Jesus, His disciples, the early-Church heroes, etc.—who have rocked the exact same frames.

If you haven't guessed by now, the frames I'm talking about are the gospel of Jesus Christ. You may get tired of hearing me say it, but there is no life outside the truth of the good news of Jesus Christ. It is the foundation, structure, and substance of *every* aspect of our lives. There is nothing you can ever do and nowhere you can ever go where it is not completely and utterly *true* and *relevant*. If we really want to see everything He intends for us to experience in the world of sports and beyond, we must fight like crazy to keep the frames on our faces.

If the frames were forged long ago by God Himself through the sweat and blood of His Son Jesus, the lenses are a somewhat newer creation.

Although I used my lenses through my many years as an athlete, these lenses were sharpened and brought into focus through my interactions with fellow brothers-in-Christ named Robbie Trent and Wes Neal. Robbie and Wes serve with the Fellowship of Christian Athletes in Nebraska and have put words to the truths that God had pounded into my heart over my years on the field. As all good authors, coaches, and preachers do, I have borrowed Robbie's and Wes' ideas, integrated them into the language of my heart, and used them as the lenses for our glasses.

As you look at the lenses, you'll see that they are each divided into four different sections, like the foursquare court we spent so much time on in elementary school. Conveniently (and intentionally!), the four quadrants converge in the middle of the lens to form the shape of a cross, placing it right in the middle of your field of vision no matter what you are doing. If you look closer, you'll notice that the four sections each have a faint outline of a letter etched into them: G.W.A.M. This acronym represents the four principles of Robbie and Wes' "Doing Sports God's Way" framework that have so resonated in my heart: Goal. Winning. Audience. Motivation. [1]

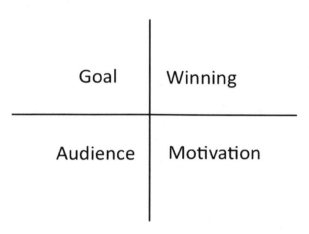

Far from being rocket science or a magic formula, I have found that these simple principles draw a big circle around competition (and life), providing for us a language and way of thinking through which to categorize and understand our experiences in the world of sports and beyond. They serve as a lens (how convenient!) for us to see our hearts and the competition that so shapes them in the way I believe Jesus does. Even though they are somewhat elementary terms that you could probably define without the help of a dictionary, they have been so beneficial to me that I would love to unpack them for you. Okay, feel free to tear into the package! Let's open it up together!

\

__TRAINING TIME__

1. Do you feel like you are viewing competition (and life) through the frames of the gospel?
2. Why do you look at sports and life the way you do?
3. What comes to mind first when you hear the *Doing Sports God's Way* principles of Goal, Winning, Audience, and Motivation?
4. What application of the truths of this chapter do you want to make in your life?

---

[1] Robbie Trent and Wes Neal, *Doing Sports God's Way*, http://nebraskafca.org/resources/dsgw1/

10

GOAL

So we make it our goal to please him, whether we are at home in the body or away from it.

—2 CORINTHIANS 5:9

And let us run with perseverance the race marked out for us, fixing our eyes on Jesus, the pioneer and perfecter of faith.

—HEBREWS 12:1-2

1076. These four digits became a rallying cry for the Furman Baseball team this past season. Everything they did—from the locker room bulletin board, to posts on social media, and to warm-up shirts—contained the same message: 1076. They even had the team goal of running 1076 trips up and down the big hill behind the track before the end of the season! Even though I am not a member of the team, it didn't take me long to realize that the number was very important to the men on the diamond. It had become a focal point, a singular and driving purpose.

And what does 1076 mean, you ask? It's the distance in miles between Furman's baseball stadium and Omaha, Nebraska, the site of the College Baseball World Series. The team had their mind set on one goal: make it to the big dance... and win it all!

What is the Goal?

Everything we do in life has a goal. If you are lifting weights, the goal is to get stronger. If you are on a diet, the goal is to lose weight. If you are taking dance lessons, the goal is to be able to break it down more successfully at the next wedding. The goal is what you rally around when things get tough. It is what causes you to lay awake at night and what causes you to get up before the sun and run stadiums until you throw up. It is the word (or number!) that is scrawled on the piece of paper and pinned to the bulletin board of your heart that drives you when nothing else can. It is the top of the mountain. The last rep. The finish line.

If everything we do in life has a goal, what is the goal of competition? Why do you compete? I can assure you that the world, SportsCenter, and every recruiting website on the internet will gladly give you an answer to that question. Here are some of the ways many athletes would answer this question:

- "To get the ring!"
- "To get a scholarship!"
- "To get girls!"
- "To be famous!"
- "To leave a legacy!"
- "To prove to my Dad that I'm not a worthless pansy."

As you heard in my story, I've heard and, even worse, chased every one of these goals. I probably even held each of these motivations deep within my heart at the same time. As you can imagine, it was just like trying to score on and defend multiple soccer nets at the same time. Impossible. I needed to see competition through God's eyes. Why did *He* have me on this field? What was *His* goal for me as I lived and competed as an athlete?

God's Goal

As recorded in the Bible, a man named Paul wrote many letters to the different churches of his day. He was an athlete—or, at least, a sports fan—who was known to use athletic images to illustrate his points for his listeners. Paul was a man who could stand between the world of athletic competition and the world of everyday life and speak definitively about God's goal for His children in each arena.

In the eighth chapter of his letter to the Church in Rome, Paul lays out God's goal and desire for His children:

> For God knew his people in advance, and he chose them to *become like his Son*, so that his Son would be the firstborn among many brothers and sisters. (Romans 8:29, NLT)

To break it down for you, God's ultimate goal for you, me, and all of His children is that we would "become like His Son" Jesus. The top of the mountain, the end of the race, and the championship ring that would define and drive us would be that we'd look, talk, walk, love, and live in such a way that we would look like Jesus. God sent Jesus to show us how to live. He wants us to keep fighting the good fight until we look exactly like Him. Jesus *knew* God intimately, and He listened to His voice every day, doing His best to obey. His life was lived for others. In the end, He gave up His life for God's Kingdom.

Of course, without the gospel and the Holy Spirit, this is impossible. But if your lens is seated firmly in the framework and hope of the gospel, God's living Spirit inside of you can help you to pursue this goal God has for you. We will never live, move, talk, and walk exactly like Jesus here on Earth, but that doesn't mean we get a free pass to not give it our all. Just because you might not play softball in the Olympics one day doesn't mean you shouldn't pour your heart and soul into being the best high school player you can possibly be. The goal is clear; our call is to go after it!

You may be wondering, "Was Paul laying out God's goal for me as an athlete or for me as an everyday person?" That is a good question. But if I could translate it, I believe it would sound more like this:

> That sounds good and all, and I can see how that would apply to my life at work or at church, but there must be something more for when I step on the court. God has an

extra set of goals for us athletes... right? Are you sure He doesn't want us to look like Jesus on Sunday *and* do whatever it takes to win the state championship? It sounds too simple to say that the *only* goal of competition is that we would look more like Jesus. What about the stats, the fame, and the rings?

I can't tell you the number of times I have asked those same questions. We could be in the middle of an undefeated season or grunting it out during off-season conditioning, but like a mosquito on a hot summer's day, these lies still pestered me. I call them "lies" because that is what they are.

ONE You, ONE Goal

The truth is that there is only *one* God and only *one* you. He knew you before you were born, and He'll know you after you leave this earth. His heart and desire for us is unwavering: "I want you to become just like my Son Jesus." This goal for us doesn't change when we put on cleats and hear the starter's gun any more than putting a coat and hat on a dog and taking him to a movie makes him a human. The dog is still a dog, and you are still God's prized, beloved child no matter what you find yourself doing.

Like the struggle I shared with living a fractured life of sin, sports, and God, the world pushes us to compartmentalize our lives like a cafeteria tray so that one area doesn't spill over into the others and create a mess. When we buy into this way of living, we naturally create different rules for the different sections of our lives. We eat the salad with a fork, the cornbread with our hands, and the pudding with our spoon. And we struggle to find a common thread to connect them all. According to Scripture and the offensive-lineman eating habits of my past, what we need is not a neat, divided cafeteria tray but rather a big bowl to mix everything together in. Once everything is touching everything else, we should grab a big wooden spoon and get after it!

God desires for us to live lives of wholeness. He doesn't just want your heart when you are cleaned up and sitting in the second pew at church. He wants it when you are covered in dirt and sweat late in the ninth inning. He loves you, and being the good Father He is, He is able to use *every* area of your life—especially competition—to move you toward His ultimate goal and desire for you: that you would become *just like* His Son.

__TRAINING TIME__

1. What is your goal as a competitor? What is your goal in life?
2. How does your goal compare with God's goal for our lives? Is one greater or deeper than the other?
3. How is God challenging you to look more like Jesus as an athlete, coach, or parent?
4. What application of the truths of this chapter do you want to make in your life?

11

WINNING

But be sure to fear the LORD and serve him faithfully with all your heart; consider what great things he has done for you.

—1 SAMUEL 12:24

Stand firm, and you will win life.

—LUKE 21:19

IN SPORTS, WINNING IS PRETTY DARN IMPORTANT. Before the 1956 Rose Bowl, UCLA head football coach Red Sanders coined the motto, "Winning isn't everything. It's the only thing."[1] While it sounds shocking at first, I really don't think anyone was surprised to hear him say that. From the beginning of time, humans have competed, and there has nearly always been a winner and a loser.

The Mayans would play a ball game where the winners were showered with gifts and the losers were executed.

Civil War generals competed for days over a single piece of land while many lay dead and dying on the field.

Every little league baseball field has a scoreboard and a champion at the end of the season.

From music to movies, we are constantly reminded, "Two is not a winner and three nobody remembers" and "If you ain't first, you're last."[2]

Everywhere you look, the message is the same: WIN… And with all the recent allegations of performance-enhancing drugs sweeping from Olympic sprinters to professional cyclists to Major League Baseball players, it's not too much of a stretch to tack on… AT ALL COSTS!

Winning in the Word

Winning is pretty important in the Bible, too. Scripture refers to our lives as a "race" or a "fight" so often that sometimes I wonder if I need to stretch before reading my Bible! I've always known that there is no better place to learn the deep truths of life than in the arena of competition. Much to my delight, God seems to feel the same way. Remember Paul, a heroic champion for God's Kingdom... a man who ran the race and fought the fight well? He challenged the Jesus followers of his day with statements such as these:

> But one thing I do: Forgetting what is behind and *straining* toward what is ahead, I *press on* toward the goal to **win** the prize for which God has called me heavenward in Christ Jesus. (Philippians 3:13-14).

> Do you not know that in a race all the runners run, but only one gets the prize? ***Run in such a way as to get the prize.*** (2 Corinthians 9:24)

And in case you are tempted to think that the world is more insistent about the importance of winning, look at what Paul says a little later:

> Everyone who competes in the games goes into *strict training*. They do it to get a crown that will not last, but we do it to get a crown that will last forever. Therefore I do not run like someone running aimlessly; I do not fight like a boxer beating the air. No, *I beat my body* and make it my slave so that after I have preached to others, I myself will not be disqualified for the prize. (2 Corinthians 9:25-27)

Paul's insistence on strict training, intense focus, and beating his body all for the sake of winning the race make me think that God was using him to urge His children to do something that sounds familiar from the world sports: WIN… AT ALL COSTS!

Defining Terms

You're probably thinking what I'm thinking: "If the world and the Bible both urge us to 'win at *all* costs', then what seems to be the problem?" Great question! After examining the evidence, it seems that desiring to win isn't the sticking point, so it must lie somewhere else. That "somewhere else" is in how we define *winning*.

How would you complete the following sentence? "Winning is _____." Just like many of our previous questions, the prevailing sports culture of our day is quick to offer its opinion and definition. A scan of any sports channel or magazine will scream back to you, "Winning is scoring more points than the other team." As we drill deeper, we find that figuring out the winner and loser of a contest isn't so difficult. You can even do it on your phone the next morning over a bowl of cereal. So if the world clearly defines *winning* as having a better score on the board at the end of the game and calls us to go after it at *all* costs, what would be the "win" that God is calling us to lay our lives down for? Are they one and the same? If not, how different are they? Can they play together, or do you have to choose one or the other? Let's find out!

The Ultimate Win

Before we go any further, let's be clear that the ultimate win and the only way to be a true champion is to know God. The only way we can know God is through believing in and building our lives upon the truth of His gospel, plain and simple. There can be no victory without Jesus just like there can be no glasses without the frame. With this in mind, let's get back to the business of discovering how God defines winning.

God's Definition

The first thought is simple. Just like every team starts out the season with a goal, God has one incredible goal for your life: that you would become like His Son Jesus. As the season progresses, every team measures their performance in light of their goal. If their performance moves them closer to their goal, it is considered a win. If it takes them farther from their goal, it is considered a loss. In college football, one of our goals was to end the season with a positive takeaway-to-turnover ratio. After every game, we would evaluate our performance as it related to this particular goal. If we recovered two fumbles and only lost one, we celebrated... until the running backs coach chimed in and said we should *never* fumble the ball.

The same holds true in our relationship with God. If our actions, attitudes, and efforts moved us closer to our goal of becoming more like Jesus, we should celebrate a victory. But if our actions, attitudes, and efforts make us look less like Jesus in the locker room mirror after the game, we should chalk it up as a loss and head back to the drawing board. Just like film from last week's game, the process of evaluating ourselves after each contest can help us begin to see areas in our game that we need to continue to fully surrender to God.

Our friend Paul begins to color in God's definition of *winning* for us through this challenge in the third chapter of the letter he wrote to the Church in Colossae:

> Whatever you do, work at it with all your heart, as working
> for the Lord, not for man. (Colossians 3:23)

It's almost as if Paul is trying to complete our fill-in-the-blank sentence from earlier! If we stand on the foundation of the gospel and then move through the filter of evaluating our performance in light of the goal of becoming more like Jesus, a pretty safe conclusion to the Bible's definition of winning could be this: "Winning is... whatever you do, work at it with all your heart, as working for the Lord, not for man."

If your entire life has been painted with the brush of the sports world like mine has, I'm sure that alarms instantly started going off in your head after you read the last sentence. Your mind is probably racing with images of coaches in flip-flops saying, "Everyone is a winner!" This mentality may cause you to imagine football games where tackling is replaced with gentle pats on the back. You probably have a million questions like, "How will we figure out who wins the game?" Or this one: "Is there a championship ring for going undefeated in God's eyes? How will anyone know that I was successful?" Maybe you're wondering, "What happens if the Bible's scoreboard and the one at the field don't match up?"

You probably smiled and nodded when we talked earlier about God's goal for competition, but things start to get a little bit crazy when we start messing with the very thing that sports has always been about for you: winning. This is one of the critical moments in our journey together where you will have to decide if you really believe that there is a fundamental difference between the way that God and the world view sports. When it all boils down, do you believe that God has a deeper reality behind the jerseys, whistles, and scoreboards? Or is what you see what you get? You decide.

If you have decided that there might be something more and you are willing to keep journeying together, let's dive deeper into how God would define this part of our lens called "winning."

Two Winners and a Loser

Jesus told a story one time about three dudes who had a chance to win (Matthew 25:14-30). Here's my take on it. They worked for a business owner who was going off on a long trip. Before the man left, he called all of them aside and entrusted his money to them. He gave five bags of gold to the first servant, two bags of gold to the second servant, and one bag of gold to the third servant. Now, before you get bent out shape and start wondering why the first guy got more, know that the Bible says the business owner knew these servants well and that he entrusted each of them with what he knew they could handle according to their abilities.

After a long time, the business owner finally returned home. He climbed down off his camel, poured the sand out of his shoes, and called his servants in to catch up on how things went while he was gone. After some hugs and a few souvenirs he had brought back from the faraway land, the business owner looked at the first servant and said, "Well, how'd it go?"

The first servant could hardly contain his excitement! He reached around the bookshelf and pulled out not five but ten bags of gold! He said, "Look! Praise God! I took *all* of the money you gave me and put it to work. It was hard. I lost some at the beginning, but I pushed and worked… and look what I ended up with: ten bags of gold! Thank you so much for trusting me enough to give me the opportunity to watch over your gold while you were gone. Here it is!"

With tears in his eyes, the business owner smiled at the man kneeling before him. He put his hand on his shoulder and gently whispered, "Listen carefully. I have hundreds of servants, but I chose to trust you with my wealth… and five bags of it at that. And you did exactly what I needed you do with them: put them in the game. I am so proud of you right now that I can hardly see straight. Well done!" His voice began to rise as he literally lifted the man to his feet. "Well done! Well done, my good and faithful servant! You have been faithful with a few things. I will put you in charge of many things! Come and give me a hug!" The business owner and servant embraced like teammates celebrating a Super Bowl win… only without the confetti, of course!

While all this was going on, the second and third servants had been watching attentively, anticipating their turn with the boss. Once the first servant left to assume his new role and responsibility, the business owner called the second servant by name. With trembling hands, he scrambled for his bags of gold and bowed before his master. As he explained to the business owner the magnificent ways he had invested the two bags of gold—which he had doubled to four—the business owner was again smiling from ear to ear. The story played out exactly like it did for the first faithful servant, and the second servant was escorted away to become familiar with his new realm of responsibility.

The business owner was so excited that his servants whom he loved dearly did such an amazing job embracing the responsibilities he had given to them that he didn't notice the look on the third servant's face as he approached. Before he could even finish asking him how it went, the third servant slid a dirty, wrinkled, musty bag of gold toward the business owner. Confused, the boss asked, "Is that what I think it is?"

The servant replied, "Yep, that's your bag of gold... just the way you gave it to me... only a little dustier. I even counted it this morning to make sure none of it had fallen out." The servant continued. "I know that you are ruthless and selfish and that you don't treat others fairly. So I was afraid and went out and dug a hole behind the shed and hid your gold in the ground. I'm sorry it got dirty, but I promise it's all there!"

Although it broke his heart, the business owner knew exactly what was happening. He had been watching that servant for a while, observing him as he went about his daily tasks. He thought he had seen something special in him. Because the servant was still young, the business owner only gave him one bag of gold, but he hoped and prayed every night of his journey that he would return home and find that his servant had been faithful. He wanted so badly to train and teach him so that, one day, he might become head over all his servants. But he had failed the test. Instead of rejoicing in the opportunity to take the business owner's stuff and "put it in the game," the servant let his fear of failing and disappointing his boss keep him from ever getting off the bench.

Although he was saddened that his servant had such a broken view of him, the business owner did what every good leader must inevitably do; he ordered his guards to take the bag of gold from him and give it to the one who had ten and then toss him off the premises. In essence, the business owner told the servant, "If you aren't going to run the ball, I'm going to have to give it to someone who will."

So, what was the score at the end of the story? When the dust had settled on the field of competition, how many of the servants won, and how many lost? As the scoreboard operator of this particular match, I believe that Jesus would hang a "2" on one side and a "1" on the other. The first two servants were clearly winners while the third was a loser. It seems obvious from the business owner's reaction, but I believe that there is something lying just beneath the exterior of the story that will bring us great freedom.

Faithful vs. Fearful

I've always thought that the business owner was happy with the first two servants and that they were winners because they took his money and increased it by 100%. Not only were they winners *internally* because of their faithfulness, they were also winners *externally* because of the results they achieved on the field. I can't tell you how many times I used this framework to measure my athletic performances. My internal dialogue would go a little something like this...

"Was I faithful? Did I leave it all on the field?"

"Yes! I fought my guts out for four quarters...Winner!"

"Was I wildly successful, and did I 'double up' through my performance?"

"Even though we won, I did give up that one sack and miss the linebacker on that draw play... Loser!"

Or...

"Was I faithful? Did I put it *all* in the game?"

"No... I went half-speed the whole second half and spent more time thinking about what I and the guys were going to do after the game... Loser!"

"Did I perform well on the field?"

"Oh, yeah! That guy was a 98-pound freshman scrub. I could have whipped him with my eyes closed. *And* we won the game 76-40... Winner!

I would still be stuck in limbo between those two competing lenses if God hadn't reminded me of what the third servant said to the master. While he was explaining why he had buried the money in the mud instead of putting it to work, the third servant said,

> I know that you are a hard man, harvesting where you have
> not sown and gathering where you have not scattered seed.

So I was afraid and went out and hid your gold in the ground. (Matthew 25:24-25)

To paraphrase, the servant said,

I've heard you are a tough coach and that you exercise complete authority over this program. And, to be honest with you, I was scared. I didn't really know what would happen if I put everything I had into the game. I figured it would be safer and probably make you happier if I just hung back and didn't risk failing.

To me, that's like saying,

Coach, I know you recruited me to be a starting pitcher, but instead of taking the ball onto the field, I think it would be a better idea if I left it in my locker and sat next to the water cooler in the dugout. That way, it will be impossible for me to give up a home run or walk somebody, *and* you won't even have to wash my uniform after the game! Whaddya think?

This is just me talking, but when I listen to Jesus' story about the three competitors, I see a distinct line drawn down the middle of the action. On one side of the line is *faithfulness*, taking everything God has entrusted to you and putting it on the line… putting it to work… putting it in the game.

On the other side of the line is *fear*, holding back what God has so graciously and intentionally entrusted to you because of fear that you might lose it… that it might not work out the way you think it should… that you might fail. Imagine if the first servant had come back to the business owner and said,

I took the five bags of gold you gave me and worked my butt off. I researched, studied, strategized, and made the best possible decision I could. But just after I invested in the lumber industry, there was a huge forest fire, and I lost most of your money. I know I only have two bags to give back to you, but I promise you that I put my heart and soul into investing what you gave me.

If that had happened, I believe the outcome would have been the same. That servant and the business owner would have celebrated together as the words "Well done, my good and faithful servant!" echoed throughout the workplace. I'm firmly convinced that all the business owner wanted was for them to realize that they had been chosen by him for a special opportunity and to work wholeheartedly to be faithful to put what he had given them in the game.

This is not at all to say that the external outcome isn't significant. The business owner would have lost three bags of gold for goodness sake! But the story does seem to reveal that God is more concerned with the scoreboard of our heart—where we can control our attitude, effort, and actions—than He is with the scoreboard above the stadium where so many things take place that are so far outside of our control. Can you be a winner in both? Of course. If you win in the heart, maxing out the talents and abilities that God gave you, will it translate to greater success in the arena of competition? Most likely. Do we get a special seat in God's Kingdom if we go undefeated in our hearts *and* win the World Series? I don't think so... but we'll have to wait and see!

Put it in the game!

The area of "competition" is a crucial battleground on which we must confront the enemy of our souls. Like I said before, you must decide if God had something deeper in mind than filling up a scoreboard when He created competition.

To put it simply, God has given to all of us unique talents and abilities. Do you want to know how I know that God gave them to us? Because, if I had been the one giving them out, I would have made myself 6'8", 340 pounds with a 4.9 forty, and I'd *still* be playing in the League!

In reality, I topped out at 6'3", 294 pounds with a 5.3 forty. And in case you are wondering, I didn't even play one down in the NFL!

God made us all special and different. His Word says He was the one who put you together in your mother's womb (Psalm 139:13). God doesn't make mistakes, and He is not careless with where He entrusts His gifts. If you can throw a spiral, it's a gift from God. If you can hit home runs, it's a gift from God. If you can bend it like Beckham, it's a gift from God. Every good thing comes from Him, and you have been given a specific amount that He wants to see you max-out on every play (James 1:17). He longs for wholehearted faithfulness, not fear.

In closing, God's definition of winning would seem to go something like this:

> *Winning* is taking the talents and abilities that God has given to you and laying them all on the line… every play… as you trust the gospel and fight to live and compete like Jesus.

TRAINING TIME

1. Before reading this chapter, how would you have completed the sentence, "Winning is _____?" How about *after* reading?
2. Do you think winning is important to God? Why or why not?
3. Where is it most difficult to apply God's definition of winning to your life?
4. What application of the truths of this chapter do you want to make in your life?

[1] Overman, Steven J. "'Winning isn't Everything. It's the Only Thing': The Origin, Attributions and Influence of a Famous Football Quote."

[2] Nelly –*Number 1; Talladega Nights*

12

AUDIENCE

Am I now seeking the approval of man, or of God? Or am I trying to please man? If I were still trying to please man, I would not be a servant of Christ.

—COLOSSIANS 1:10

Whatever you do, work at it with all your heart, as working for the Lord, not for man.

—COLOSSIANS 3:23

WHEN YOU COMPETE, you *always* have an audience. No matter what sport you are playing, the audience is always there. Whether it is the tiny group of parents huddled under one umbrella to watch the finish of your cross-country meet or if it is a sellout crowd at the state championship game, they are there. The eyes and faces of the faithful provide a silent and, sometimes, not-so-silent backdrop to your athletic competition. They roar in approval when you win, and they sigh and, sometimes, yell in disgust when you lose. Even though every sports psychologist has tried for years, there is no way to separate the crowd from the game. They are inseparably linked in a way that is weaved into the very fabric of sport.

I believe this is part of God's brilliance in designing competition. He knew that we were hardwired to live and compete for an audience, so He gave us the athletic arena to put this into practice. Think about it.

If you spend all your time alone hitting in the batting cage in your backyard or playing basketball on your own in the church gym, you will never learn how to play for someone other than yourself. You will be your worst critic and your greatest fan, but the lessons and voices you learn and hear will be found only inside your head. There will be no audience there to provide feedback, encouragement, or challenge. Where else can you get such complete and instant feedback on your performance? During our wrestling matches in high school, I could have closed my eyes and told you whether my teammate won or lost based solely on the response of the crowd!

If we believe that competition is God's testing ground and classroom for His children, I believe that a lesson He desperately wants to teach us is *which audience to play for.*

If God wants to teach us which audience to play for, what does that even mean? Does He mean only play in front of the friendly home crowd and sit out the games in front of the crazies at our rival school? Is there an ideal size of audience? How do you even pick your audience anyway? Good questions!

Before we can begin to answer the question of who to play for, we must take a closer look at who is in our audience. Follow me...

Who is in the stands?

In high school, we battled our crosstown rivals in front of 26,000 folks in the big, old stadium downtown. In college, I had the opportunity to play football in front of 83,000 screaming people dressed in orange at Clemson University my senior year. There were 350 people at our wedding to witness one of the greatest underdog victories of all time when my wife said, "I do!" However, all of this pales in comparison to the audiences of some of our professional sports.

The Dallas Cowboys can fit 111,000 spectators in their new stadium. One billion people watched the 2008 opening ceremonies for the Beijing Olympics, and 3.2 billion (46.4% of the World's Population!) tuned in to watch the 2010 FIFA World Cup![1] Are these the audiences God is wanting us to compete for? We'll see. Let's keep going.

The Best Audience

Think about your own experiences with competition as we wrestle through these questions. Out of all the people in the audience, how many of them really know you? How many of them could outline the goals the team laid out before the season? How many of them would define winning the same way you do? How many of them were at practice with you earlier this week when you had a fever and it took every ounce of strength simply to finish? Again… out of all the people in your audience, how many of them *really* know you? If I had to answer these questions about my audiences during competition, the bleachers would quickly fade away, and I would be left with my coach and a handful of teammates as the only ones I could answer these questions positively for.

The only ones who can even *begin* to evaluate your performance on anything more than some numbers on a scoreboard are the ones who are closest to you, the ones who know what you're standing on and how much you have laid on the line to get where you are… the ones who know your *heart*. And out of that group, the only one who sat in your living room on a recruiting visit, who rejoiced with you when you signed with the team, who studied you and the game tirelessly to be able to put you in the best position to make a play, who loved you enough to stay after practice and work on sharpening your specific skills, and who has a history with the game to be able to speak authoritatively about any situation is… your coach.

Having played sports my whole life—in many different settings and in front of many different people—I would argue that, if I was going to pick an audience to play for, I wouldn't drum up the massive crowds filling the stadium seats. And as much as I love them, I wouldn't even look to my teammates. Instead, I would zero-in on playing for one person: my coach. It just makes sense! For all the reasons listed above and a hundred more, the logical choice seems to be to pour all of our effort into competing for the pleasure of our head coach.

So, before you start jumping up and down and telling me how much you don't like your head coach and how it would be a much better idea to play for your girlfriend, your teammates, the janitor, or anyone else…

let me tell you, like I mentioned before, that *God* wants to be your head coach.

If athletics and our spiritual lives are as intimately linked as I believe they are, He has created the position of head coach to teach us more about Himself and how He desires to lead us through this life. Think about it. He recruited us, threw a party when we joined His team, created us with specific talents and abilities, and knows the game plan from beginning to end. He never loses focus on the goal and is able to coach us through difficult situations because He's been there before. He is the perfect coach, and He wants to be your audience of one.

Paul's statement to the Church at Colossae that we looked at in the previous section makes God's desire crystal clear: "Whatever you do, work at it with all your heart, *as working for the Lord, not for man.*"

Do what? Everything.

How? With *all* your heart.

For who? For the pleasure of your Heavenly Coach… not for anybody else.

Audience of ONE

Just imagine it… It's your senior year, and you've trained like crazy for your final track season. Your coach personalized off-season workouts for you that had you in peak physical condition. You lost tons of sweat over the summer, ran through the leaves in the fall, and even bundled up to put in work during the winter. You were ready! There are no words to describe how incredible the season has been. You have won every race by at least two seconds, and the local newspaper has started following your every move of their new "queen of the track." Last week, you even had an interview on the radio! More and more people have been showing up at the meets to see their "local hero" run. Even your opponents have begun to stare at you in awe as you take the blocks.

You've been handling it all pretty well, but you must admit that you kind of like the attention. You love the swell of pride and burst of adrenaline you get when the crowd roars your name as you round the last turn, and the cute boys who wave at you as you warm up aren't too bad either.

AUDIENCE

Your coach—a humble, focused woman named Susan Austin—has been a constant force the whole time. Coach Austin was the one who had noticed you during the mile-run in physical education class during your freshman year and urged you to try out for the track team. She had gone above and beyond the call of duty and had often stayed late to help you work on starts and turns. She had even driven you home on several occasions. Beyond all of that, she had really stepped in when your mom passed away last spring. She was a coach, but she was so much more than that.

The Monday after the final meet of the regular season, Coach Austin called you into her tiny office in the back of the locker room and said she had some good news for you. You played it cool as she told you that you had qualified for the state meet later that week, but inside, you were doing cartwheels! She winked and said, "See you this afternoon, Champ", as you turned to walk out. That afternoon's workout was a breeze. You were already riding the wave of emotion as you anticipated the size of the crowd, the sound of your name coming from the stands as you rounded turn four, and the weight of the medal around your neck.

You were rehearsing your answers for the reporters when Coach Austin called you over and told you there had been a mistake. She said, "I can't remember anything like this in my 34 years of coaching, but they've accidentally admitted one too many runners into the field at State. When they asked me what I thought they should do, I convinced them to let you run your race here before the state meet. Because I've been on the state board for 20 years, I guess they trust me to turn in an honest time. Besides, I told them you might even run better without all the distraction surrounding State."

As your jaw dropped, he threw in, "Why don't we do it during my planning period tomorrow? That's roughly what time of day you've been running in all the other meets this year, so that should work great!" She winked again and walked off the track.

You couldn't really sleep that night. You didn't know whether to laugh or cry, to hug Coach Austin or shove her for suggesting such a crazy setup. Either way, all you could think about as you wrestled your-self to sleep was how Coach had always been there and how she probably knew best.

Showtime!

The next day at 10:15 a.m., you got up from your desk and made your way out to the track behind the school. A few of your classmates high-fived you, but the rest went right back to their assignment. A couple of birds in a tree over by the parking lot were the only things making a sound as the sun hung in the cloudless sky. As you rounded the corner of the gym, you instantly noticed how empty the stadium felt without the audience that had filled it all season long, and a feeling in your stom-ach began to make you wonder just how much you had relied on the adrenaline boost around the fourth curve.

Before you could spiral any deeper into your thoughts, a booming voice greeted you. "Good Morning, Champ!" It was Coach Austin in her familiar track pants and worn-out shoes, holding a stopwatch and smiling from ear to ear. "You ready to do this thing?" she asked as you laced on your spikes. You looked up at her, and the confidence in her eyes suddenly lifted you to your feet. After your typical warmup routine, she put her hand on your shoulder and looked you square in the eyes. "You know the drill. Win at *all* costs. Take everything you have, and put it all on the line. I'm here with you."

Shaking back the tears, you grit your teeth and dug into the lone starting block. Coach gave you the cadence and fired the gun. You took off like a rocket and ran as hard as you ever had. Turn one… Turn two… Back straightaway… Turn three… As you rounded turn four, you could feel your body pulling against you. You had poured everything you had onto the track and needed one last burst to finish.

Your eyes darted to the stands, but they were empty. The cute guys and flashbulbs had been replaced by a couple of hot dog wrappers rolling lazily in the breeze. As soon as you were about to use up your last ounce of drive, your eyes noticed something… a lone figure standing by the finish line with her eyes locked on you. Instantly, you were filled with gratitude for everything she had done for you. Your eyes began to sting with tears because you wanted so badly to run for her… to win for her.

As you flew by her at the finish line, you heard the beep of the stopwatch and *knew* you had run your best race ever. You held nothing back and did everything exactly how Coach showed you to. There was nothing that you would have changed about your performance.

When you finally slowed down and turned around, you were surprised by how quickly Coach Austin managed to wrap you up in one of her signature bearhugs. She told you how proud of you she is and affirmed your feeling that you had just run your best race ever. As she leaned back to look at you, you could see into the depths of her heart and *knew* that you were loved and that she truly was pleased with your performance. There was a feeling inside of you that couldn't be rivaled by any medal anyone could ever put around your neck.

As you walked off the track with your coach by your side, you suddenly remembered that you never saw the stopwatch! You stopped in your tracks and asked her what your time was. All she did was wink and say, "You'll have to read about it in the papers tomorrow, Champ."

So, what do you think? How does playing for an audience of one, your coach, sound? What's *really* bouncing around in your heart right now? Would it make a difference if I told you that you set a new state record and that they threw a pep-rally downtown and gave you a key to the city the following weekend? Would it make a difference if I told you that Coach Austin went back to her office, had a stroke, and died before she could report your time… and that it was lost forever? If you were running for the right audience, as a true winner, would it really even matter?

Anybody but Coach

I have heard of folks who haven't been able to fully grasp the reality that God is their loving, Heavenly Father because of an abusive or neglectful earthly father. I think I understand that. If your sports career was anything like mine, I'm sure you have had the opportunity to play for several different coaches… some who were examples of a great head coach and others who merely used you and spit you out while cussing you like a dog. I know it can be hard to wade through all the negative experiences you have had with earthly coaches to be able to see your Heavenly Coach clearly, but if God desires to be our coach and our audience, we must try to view Him that way.

I played for coaches from across the spectrum. I had some who I would break my neck trying to catch a glimpse of while I was competing because I knew they would be looking right back at me, offering encouragement and direction. I had others who I would avoid at all costs because they had a track record of constantly heaping shame and discouragement on me. To one, I was a valuable young man to be shaped and molded. To the other, I was a mule to be whipped if I didn't perform to the exact standards of perfection. There seemed to be a fundamental difference between the coaches who cared about my heart and those who only cared about their coaching resume. The difference is clear, but I'll bet that, if you close your eyes and try to imagine God on the sidelines, you'll have to sort through all the different pictures of "coach" that are floating around in your heart. Because that is the case for all of us, let's try to sketch a picture of how our Heavenly Father would lead if He had the whistle.

I want to offer you three roles I think God plays as our coach: *Lover, Leader, and Teacher.* However, before we flesh out these roles, we need to call a 20-second timeout and make sure that God's two most foundational roles are cemented in our hearts: *Savior* and *Lord.*

God as Savior

You and I were stuck. We were dead in our sins with no way out. We were slaves to our desires and the brokenness inside of us and were doomed to live a life of chaos, apart from God forever. Jesus, God's only Son, entered our disgusting brokenness, lived a perfectly sinless life, and willingly submitted Himself to death on a cross to pay for the sins of the world. God brought Him back to life three days later to show that death and sin had been defeated, and He rose through the clouds back to Heaven.

The Bible says that Jesus is standing at your door and knocking (think recruiting visit) and that, if you believe that He's who He says He is, your sins will be paid for and God Himself will move into the living room of your heart (Revelation 3:20). You'll be rescued from slavery to sin and death that dominated your life and sign a never-ending contract with the greatest team ever. The best part of the whole deal is that you will have free access to the head coach of the Universe, God Himself, and will get to spend the rest of your life and eternity in an amazing relationship with Him where you have the joy of having Him teach you how to run the plays that He is calling for you.

God as Lord

He's God, and you're not. He's the head coach, and you're not. He has the whistle and the playbook, and you don't. While I enjoy them every day, I believe that the vast amount of personal freedom and individualism that comes from living in a democratic society makes it difficult for us to grasp the concept of God being our Lord. We are used to having a say-so in almost everything that happens, so it is hard for us to comprehend complete authority. Fortunately for us, however, God created sports to teach us just that!

The two most powerful words in the English language are these: "Coach said…" Think about it. If Coach said be on the bus at 6:00 a.m., what time were you on the bus? 5:50! If Coach showed you how to perform a particular move, didn't you try to do it exactly how you were instructed? Absolutely. If Coach blew his whistle and told everyone to start chopping their feet, did you even hesitate? Of course, not! Who else can exert such authoritative control over the hearts and minds of 18 middle school girls on a softball team or 100 high school boys on a football team? Only the coach.

God is our head coach. What He says goes. When He says turn right, we turn right. When He says do it again, we do it again. When He pulls us aside to show us how to do a specific technique more precisely, we listen. He was there before the world began. He is making your heart beat in your chest right now. He paid the price to save you from your rotten sins, and there is no one in Heaven or on Earth who is stronger, higher, or more amazing than He is. He is Lord.

Now that we have put those two layers of foundation in place, let's continue to paint the picture of how I believe the Bible would define God's role as head coach. Remember I'm only referring to the role He would play in the life of someone who has trusted the gospel, who is on the team, and who is looking to God as his or her head coach. Just like your coach, God has a different relationship with the folks on His team than He does with those who aren't. So if you are on the team, come with me to meet your head coach! If you aren't a part of the team yet, take notes… because He is available to everyone.

God as Lover

The Bible says that "God *is* love" (1 John 4:16). Love is woven into the fabric of who He is, and it is impossible for Him to do anything that would fall outside of the playing field of love. Period. The Bible says God's love for us is what motivated Him to send Jesus to save us (John 3:16). It even goes so far as to say that the only way that we can know *true* love is by understanding the way that Jesus willingly sacrificed Himself for us on the cross (1 John 3:16). As our coach, God's primary motivation is His love for us, and He'll do whatever it takes to show you that.

So when you are in the heat of competition and the odds are quickly stacking against you, remember that the coach calling your name from the sidelines loves you. You are the reason why He coaches. The Bible says,

> The LORD your God is with you, the Mighty Warrior who saves. He will take great delight in you; in his love he will no longer rebuke you, but will rejoice over you with singing. (Zephaniah 3:17).

He is not interested in belittling you in front of the whole stadium. He is wanting to speak life and courage into your soul so you can press on and hang one more point on the scoreboard of your heart.

Now, don't misunderstand me. God's love does not make Him soft. Just because He loves you doesn't mean He won't do the difficult things necessary to achieve His goal for your life—that is, for you to become more like His Son Jesus. It only means that, as a *lover* coach, His eyes will be fixed squarely on your heart and not on some performance-based scoreboard. God has already proven how much He loves you on the cross. There is nothing you can do to make Him love you any more, and there's nothing you can screw up that will make Him love you any less. Compete in that freedom!

God as Leader

The best coaches show the path by the way they live their lives. They are not the ones who run practice from the comfort of a lounge chair and beach umbrella. They are the ones who are in the mix with their hat turned backward and sweat pouring down their face. "Do as I say and not as I do" is a foreign concept to them. They would rather stay after practice with you, toss you in their car, take you home to eat dinner with their family, help you with your homework, give you a bed to sleep in, and take you back to school in the morning than miss an opportunity for you to see what the game—and what life—is really all about.

I once overheard a high school coach say, "They've got me coaching lacrosse this spring… I don't even know what lacrosse is." How crazy to think that budget cuts would force someone to lead in an arena in which the person had no experience. The beauty of God as our leader-coach, however, is that He has been through everything we will ever go through and has left for us the perfect example of how to play the game of life. According to the Bible,

> We do not have a high priest [Jesus] who is unable to em-
> pathize with our weaknesses, but we have one who has

been tempted in every way, just as we are—yet he did not sin. (Hebrews 4:15)

He didn't just play the game. He was an undefeated All-American who actually invented the game to begin with! Because this is true, God is able to speak with authority as He coaches us both on and off the field.

I've also seen coaches who would preach self-control and responsibility on the field while their personal lives were riddled with indulgence and irresponsibility. I believe it is nearly impossible to wholeheartedly follow someone who says one thing and does another. Our brains will constantly tell us, "If they really believed it, they would be doing it too, so it can't really be that important." There is something so valuable in integrity. What you see is what you get. And I'm here to tell you that God is the only coach who will ever live up to the standards that He sets for you 100% of the time. He is perfect. He is the same yesterday, today, and forever. It is impossible for him to say one thing and do another (Hebrews 13:8). He is and always will be the only one you can fully trust to coach you with complete integrity. He is your leader-coach. Follow Him!

God as Teacher

A teacher and a coach both have the same fundamental goal: to take something that is outside of you and find a way to jam it inside of you in such a way that it changes your life forever. The English teacher seeks to improve your grasp on punctuation and grammar by teaching you the basic concepts and then taking you through exercises designed to help you internalize the lesson. The coach teaches in the same way, only punctuation and grammar are replaced by hitting, catching, and throwing. If you blur your eyes, they really start to become one in the same: the *teacher-coach*.

One of the subtle differences between a coach and, say, a history teacher is the ability of the coach to go to extreme measures to make the lesson stick in the minds of his or her students. I've had some teachers do some crazy things in the name of learning, but none of them made us meet in the stadium at 6:00 a.m. and run until we puked. That special tool is reserved for the coach! Remember in the movie *Facing the Giants* when the coach made the defensive captain bear-crawl 100 yards with another human on his back? Just another example of how the coach has a special freedom to go to lengths to prove a point that would get a "normal" teacher fired.

The teacher-coach is always designing his lessons strategically to move his players one step closer to their goal. He is also keenly aware of the team's win-loss record and each individual player's performance. He tailors drills, practice schedules, and individual interactions to meet these real-life needs. If the goal of sports is to "win at all costs," the teacher-coach is constantly assessing his athletes and dreaming up ways to give them what they need to win.

Likewise, if God's goal for His athletes is "to become more like His Son Jesus," you'd better believe He is dead set on using every trick in the book to help us achieve it.

One of God's greatest teaching tools to help us achieve the goal of becoming like Jesus is discipline. All too often in our culture, that word draws to mind negative pictures of a coach choking a player, throwing chairs around the gym, or chucking basketballs at people's heads. It seems way harder than it should be to come up with examples of coaches who lovingly use discipline to teach their players that the only way to achieve their goal is by living within the rules of the team.

Two men pop into my mind when I think about a teacher-coach lovingly using discipline to shape his players. The first is Super Bowl Champion Coach Tony Dungy. He never yelled or screamed at his players but chose rather to teach them through each situation. Far from being a pushover, one of his players said he knew Coach Dungy was really upset when he would lower his voice and pull you in close to highlight where you missed the mark.[2]

The second man who comes to mind is Matt Reeves. Matt played football at Clemson, runs an incredible inner-city center, and could go toe-to-toe with any human alive on the wrestling mat. He is also a teacher-coach. While fulfilling his duties as "Mean Dean" at a camp we

were both working one summer, I overheard him say to one of the camp-
ers who was being disciplined for sneaking out of his dorm room, "I love
ya, but you've got to learn to follow the rules." Oh, and did I mention
that it was midnight and that the camper was covered in throw-up and
grass clippings from having just log-rolled the length of the football
field? It was a sincere lesson aimed at the heart of the young man but
administered through one of the coach's greatest tools: discipline.

The Bible encourages us to see the hard times in our lives as discipline that God is using to teach us to be more like Jesus. It says, "No
discipline seems pleasant at the time, but painful [I love how honest the
Bible is!]. Later on, however, it produces a harvest of righteousness and
peace for those who have been trained by it" (Hebrews 12:11). It even
goes on to say that, if God is not disciplining you, you are not truly His
child. Think about it. Do coaches make their own players or players
from the opposing team do pushups for dropping a pass? God loves you,
He has given you an example to follow, and He will go to any means
necessary to help you learn how to be more like Jesus. He is the ultimate
teacher- coach.

The Complete Picture

You are *always* competing in front of an audience, and that's a good
thing. God made it that way so we would learn to look outside of ourselves for encouragement, guidance, and feedback. We were not designed to live, work, and compete in solitary isolation. However, when
we begin to study our audience, we start to realize that only a handful of
people in it are eligible to give us feedback and guidance at the level that
we really need it... the heart level. There is only one person who is ultimately qualified to speak authoritatively to the very depth of our heart:
our coach.

The gospel, the entire Bible, and especially Paul's words to the Colossians make it clear that, not only has God designed sport and coaching to teach us more about our relationship with Him, He desires to be
our one and only audience and our one and only head coach. He is the
only one who has been there since the beginning, the only one who can

see into the depths of your heart, and the only one who died to show you exactly how much He loves you. As your coach, He will be your perfect Savior, Lord, Lover, Leader, and Teacher. He is dying for you to live and compete solely for His pleasure.

Let me be completely clear. This is one of the hardest things you will ever do. As I detailed earlier, my life has been constantly dominated by having my eyes on the wrong audience. I have played and lived to make the crowd happy, and I have often missed the gentle voice of my coach in the middle of my antics. This is not easy, but it will change your life. Listen one more time, and hold tightly to this command:

> Whatever you do, work at it with all your heart, *as working for the Lord, not for man*.

Now, go do it.

One of my greatest encouragements to do this well has come from a little section from the book of *Hebrews*. I have memorized this, and I think it would do you well to do the same! It has been like ammunition for my soul. Here it is. Get it in you!

> Therefore, since we are surrounded by such a great cloud of witnesses, let us *throw off* everything that hinders and the sin that so easily entangles. And let us run with perseverance the race marked out for us, *fixing our eyes on Jesus*, the pioneer and perfecter of faith. For the joy set before him He endured the cross, scorning its shame, and sat down at the right hand of the throne of God. Consider him who endured such opposition from sinners, *so that you will not grow weary and lose heart*. (Hebrews 12:1-3)

Fix your eyes on Jesus! Run the race!

__TRAINING TIME__

1. What was the best audience you have ever competed in front of? What made it so special?
2. What comes to mind when you hear that God wants to be your head coach? Do you have any baggage associated with someone in that position in your life?
3. What would be different about the way you compete and live if you did everything for an audience of one?
4. What application of the truths of this chapter do you want to make in your life?

---

[1] FIFA.com

[2] Tony Dungy, *Quiet Strength*

13

MOTIVATION

Love always protects, always trusts, always hopes, always perseveres.

—1 CORINTHIANS 13:7

For Christ's love compels us, because we are convinced that one died for all.

—2 CORINTHIANS 5:14

AS YOU'VE PROBABLY NOTICED BY NOW, these concepts we have been wrestling through are not easy. They will constantly leave you swimming upstream against a polluted and broken sports culture that is adamant it has found the path to life. It will take a supernatural effort to hold your ground and fight forward as you live and compete for God. And when you get knocked down, you are going to need some rock-solid motivation in order to keep getting back up.

As competitors, I guarantee that we can all remember that one motivational speech that grabbed hold of our soul and caused us to kick it into another gear as we faced our opponent in the second half. And I guarantee we can also remember a handful of times when the "motivational" pep talk missed the mark and left us shaking our heads as we geared ourselves up for the field.

I remember hearing in high school that the coach of one of our conference rivals would motivate his team by doing some pretty weird things. Before one game, he brought out a potato and a plastic drinking straw and set them on a stool in front of the team. As he circled the locker room, he asked, "How many of you think I can jam that straw through that potato?" They all scratched their heads and finally agreed that they didn't think it was possible. With a fire in his eyes (this is how I imagine it went down), he grabbed the potato and jammed the straw all the way through to the other side and shouted, "If I can put this straw through this potato, we can win the game!" Unfortunately for them, we beat them handily that Friday night, but it did give us a great idea for a banner for the next year we played them: YOUR STRAW WON'T GO THROUGH THIS POTATO!

With so many different styles and concepts of motivation floating around out there, I think it would do us some good to come to a consensus on a definition of *motivation* before we journey onward.

Motivation Defined

What is *motivation?* When I asked a group of high school athletes at a camp this question, they all generally landed in the same place: motivation is "that thing that drives you." It is the force that sits in the deep parts of you and honestly answers the question of "why" you do what you do. If you could take every action and capture it in a jar, stick it in the microwave, and boil it down to its core elements, I believe you'd discover that the motivation behind the action would be one of the items left in the bowl. It is important and inseparable from the fabric of the action itself.

Being a highly visual learner, I love to think about motivation as a picture that hangs on the wall above the fireplace in your heart, one that you have looked at a thousand times and could sketch in your sleep if you had to. If the *goal* is the word that you pin on the bulletin board and aim at every day, the *motivation* is the worn out, folded-up picture that you pull out of your wallet when people ask you why you get up so early, work so hard, and sacrifice so much to achieve your goal. It's the old photo of his wife and daughters the World War II soldier kept in his shirt pocket as he fought every day to stop the spread of evil that would jeopardize their lives and freedom. It's the image that is seared in your heart and you see when you close your eyes during off-season condition-ing. It courses through your veins and defines the very reason why you compete. It is, at every level, what *motivates* you to keep fighting.

What motivates you?

Assuming we are on the same page with the definition of motivation, let me ask you the obvious next question: "What motivates you?" Espe-cially when you are in the arena of competition, "What motivates you?" What is that thing deep inside of you that drives you to achieve your goal? Why do you do what you do? Think about it.

Did you come up with an answer? If you did, good! If not, take some time and wrestle through it. Maybe you need to lie awake tonight after everyone else has gone to bed, when it is just you and God, and ask Him to show you what picture is hanging above the fireplace in your heart. Don't be scared of what you might find. Be honest. God *loves* when we allow Him to be our tour guide as we take an honest assessment of ourselves. So, what is it? Once you get it, keep reading.

Just a quick note before we go on... If our goal is screwed up, then most likely, our motivation will be, too. It is hard to have a pure, right motivation if our goal isn't noble, godly, or biblical. Think about it. If your goal is to be the baddest dude on the block—with the most money, most women, and most drugs—then, it will be very hard for your moti-vational picture to be rated anything less than PG-13 or R. However, if your goal for competition *and* life is to become more like God's Son Jesus, it will be more likely that your motivation will fall in line with what God desires it to be. It's not a sure thing that if your goal is correct your motivation will be, too. But I can guarantee you that if your goal is off your motivation will be off as well.

So, what motivates you?

If you are anything like me (I'm not assuming you are, but I think you can find yourself somewhere in the middle of what I'm about to share), you have probably spent your life bouncing back and forth be-tween a handful of different motivations like an indecisive interior dec-orator trying to decide which painting best completes the room. For me, that has *always* been a pendulum swing between fear and pride with just a little bit of anger thrown in here and there. As much as I hate to admit it, the two pictures that have driven the bulk of my life—sports and beyond—have been pretty gross. While I am not proud of them, I think that identifying the broken, incomplete pictures I try to motivate myself with have allowed me to identify the times when I am missing the mark. Then, I can fight back to the place where God's motivation sits in its rightful place. So, for sake of illustration, let me paint the two pictures for you so you can see where *not* to find your motivation!

Fear

It was third and long, and we were down by four. We needed to score to win the game and advance to the semifinal round of the playoffs, but the ticking clock was closing the door quickly. We huddled up, and the quarterback called the play: "97 on one, on one. Ready... break!" It was a pass play with a simple hinge protection, but as I jogged to the line, all I could think about was how Rahiem had jumped me on this very play at practice earlier that week and had disrupted the quarterback. As I settled into my pass-protection stance, the voice in my head, the picture in my heart, the driving force inside of me said,

> Don't screw up. Don't screw up! Everyone is watching you. If you screw up now, it will cost your teammates the game. The fans will be upset. Oh, by the way... They'll know it was *you* who blew the play. You'll never be respected at school again. You'll never have any friends again. Coach will never trust you again. Don't screw up!

The ball snapped, and as I turned, my right hand lagged a little bit. The defensive end jumped my inside shoulder and took off like a rocket toward the quarterback. I pivoted and took off after him, but it was of no use. The quarterback, who was standing tall and looking down the field, never saw him coming and got drilled in the back by *my* man. To make matters worse, I was greeted five yards from the sideline by an irate coach who chewed me all the way to the bench and then left me to drown in my failure.

Far from a pure love for the sport and a desire to give my very best and leave the results up to God, I was instead driven by a nagging feeling in the pit of my stomach that my next mistake could be my last. A deep fear of failure and being exposed in front of everyone muscled the joy of competition out of the way and began to rot my insides, skewing the way I viewed *every* area of my life. "Succeed at all costs because failing would destroy me" was my mindset.

Pride

It was the middle of wrestling season, and we were facing a big conference match between one of our fiercest rivals. I had won the wrestle-off between the heavyweights earlier that week, so I was slated to compete at the 275-pound spot for our squad that night.

The match was back and forth, and it looked like it might come down to the result of the heavyweight bout. I paced behind the bench like a lion in a tiny cage, anticipating the moment I had prepared for. Finally, it arrived. The 215-pound match ended in victory for our school, leaving us down by five. I needed a pin to win. As I jogged over to the scorer's table to check in, I took a glance at the crowd and looked reassuringly at my parents. I wasn't sure what the outcome was going to be, but I knew I had prepared well, and I liked the thought that, if it all went my way, I could be the savior for our team. My opponent was one I hadn't pinned all season, but that didn't matter much now. As the ref blew the whistle to start the first period, we were off.

It was one of those matches that you dream about. The other guy seemed to be a little off, and everything I tried was working. From throws to snap-downs, I had my way with him. I continued to rack up take-downs and back points. Before I knew it, I was up 13-0! I knew we needed six points to win the match, so the five points we would get for me "teching" him would not be enough. (For all you non-wrestlers, a tech fall is like a run-rule in baseball. When you go up by 15 points, the match is over.) I charged at him, and hip tossed him to the ground like a rag doll. As the ref counted off the back points, I had one thought driving me: "Pin him! Do it! You will be the man, and everyone will know it was *you* who won the match for the team. Won't it feel great to have all those folks patting you on the back and congratulating you as the hero that you are? Pin him! Win the match! This is *your* time!"

I literally willed his shoulder blades to the mat. The ref's hand slapping the mat instantly validated my existence as a competitor. I did it! I was a winner! I had saved the day! As I raised my hands to the sky in victory, I let my eyes and ears soak in the self-centered celebration that I had started in the stands, on our bench, and in my heart.

Victory, the scoreboard, and the person looking back at me in the mirror had literally become my gods. In this frame of mind, no longer did I compete for the simple satisfaction of laying everything I had on the line. I was hunting like a drug addict for the next self-centered high. Not only did I miss God, but in my frenzied search to find pictures of *myself* in the paper the next day, I missed the chance to love and celebrate my teammates as well. My pride put me and what God had allowed me the incredible fortune to accomplish on the throne and threw everyone else under the bus.

Here's a freebie. For me, this one was far less frequent and far easier to define but, nonetheless, still as disgusting and dangerous.

Anger

I was having a bad day. Something inside of me was a little off as I boarded the bus to head to the stadium. I knew how badly we needed to win that night, and I let Coach's words from the pregame meal soak over me. He had reminded us what was riding on this game and how the opposing school had disrespected us in the paper earlier in the week. He even threw in a challenge of our manhood to sweeten the deal. I had listened to every word, and I was letting a storm brew inside of me. During pre-game warm ups, I stared at the opposing team and imagined how good it was going to feel to physically crush their bodies. I suddenly remembered another motivational pointer coach had delivered to us earlier in the year: "Imagine that the other team is coming after your momma. Do *whatever* it takes to stop them." This only added fuel to the fire of my anger as I pinpointed the guy who was going to line up across from me.

The game started, and I came out of the gate like a crazy man. I didn't do anything illegal or outside of the rules, but I could tell that there was something different motivating my performance. Instead of taking pleasure in the beauty of the block, I could only find pleasure in running my opponent into the ground as hard as I possibly could. The fire inside of me was screaming,

> Kill him! *Kill* him! He is your enemy, and you have been put here for one purpose: to knock him out of the game. Make sure he is in so much pain tomorrow morning that he will always remember the time when he lined up across from you. The only way to *really* play this game is with the fire of anger burning in your soul. Kill him!

I played an outstanding game. We won decisively. My opponent gave up halfway through the third quarter. I was dominant. I liked the way the fire made me play, but I wondered if I controlled it or if it was controlling me.

Playing not to lose, to glorify yourself, or to destroy your opponent are all insufficient motivations. They will leave you worn out, empty, and farther away from the ultimate goal of Christlikeness than when you started.

Does any of that sound familiar? Have you seen any of those pictures hanging in your heart? If not, what does yours look like? Take a few minutes, and draw it out. It's important to know where we are before we can exchange it for the truth.

Now that we've gone down those dark corridors and done the hard work of honestly examining ourselves, let's step back into the light to see what God desires for our true motivation to be.

His Motivation: YOU

Just a helpful hint: If you are ever wondering what you should do in a particular situation, the best place to look is always to Jesus. How did He handle Himself? What was important to Him? I know it's cliché, but seriously… what would Jesus do? Let's take a look!

Jesus and God (and the Holy Spirit) are one. They have forever existed in perfect harmony and unity, while still maintaining their unique qualities.

Think of it this way. I am one person, Scott Shuford. But at the same time, I am a son, a husband, and a father. I'm one being with three distinct roles, each with unique qualities.

Jesus is God's true Son sent from Heaven to show us exactly how to live this life. Jesus never made a mistake, never accidentally sinned, and never once chose to do anything that was not in line with God's perfect will. He is the ultimate example of what this life on Earth is supposed to look like, so it's a 100% safe assumption that His motivation is exactly what we should aspire to copy as we live and compete.

So, what was it? What was the picture that was hanging above the fireplace in the heart of God's perfect Son? From Jesus' perspective, I believe it would look something like this…

I can remember when it all began. It was so much fun getting to work to bring God's spoken Words into creation! When He said, "Let there be light!", I molded the sun with my hands like playdough. When He said, "Separate the land and the water," I carved out the deep oceans. When He spoke of the different creatures, I let my imagination run wild as I fashioned giraffes and whales and set them free in their new homes.

It was all so incredible, but one creation took our breath away: man. When He said, "Let us make mankind in our image," I could hardly contain my excitement! This was the moment we had been planning for and dreaming of. We were going to create a being who would house an eternal Spirit and rule over all of the birds in the air and the fish in the sea.

It was such a joy to walk with the man and woman in the Garden during the cool times of the morning before the sun got too hot. We would talk for hours or simply be together as they went about their work of naming the animals and working the land. There aren't enough words in any language to tell you just how much we loved those first humans! Our fellowship was so sweet, and the deep intimacy between us was almost as amazing as the oneness I enjoy with God the Father. Everything was right and good.

One day, however, something was different. As I moved down the same path I had walked every day since the beginning of humanity, Adam and Eve were nowhere to be found. I knew what had happened, and my heart was broken, but I couldn't stop myself from calling out the names of our most treasured creation: "Adam... Eve... where are you?" Slowly, they revealed their hiding places among the leaves, and the effects of their sin became instantly obvious. Their joyful, peaceful smiles had been replaced by anxious eyes darting back and forth and a posture that suggested they would rather retreat back into the weeds than stand in my presence. I longed to gather them in my arms, but their willful choice of disobedience and rebellion had damaged our once-intimate relationship. They had chosen death over life, and they knew it. As deeply as it hurt, we carried through with the consequence of their sin, and our time together as we knew it came to an end.

It ripped my heart out to watch as brother killed brother, an entire nation forgot God and worshipped idols their hands had made, and the whole world slowly destroyed itself through its unbelievable appetite for sin. Project Earth, which had begun so beautifully, was now in a full-speed nosedive toward destruction with every single human being living as a slave to sin and death. The free will that had once made our love affair with humanity so sweet had now become a noose that they were using to hang themselves with.

At just the right moment, when all hope seemed to have been lost, God the Father came to me with the plans for a mission to rescue our precious children from sin and death forever. As we talked through the specifics, I understood it wouldn't be easy. It would literally cost me everything and leave me cold, alone, and dead. But it would open a way for humanity to be rid of sin and to once again walk in sweet fellowship with us. I looked at the Father, and my love for Him consumed me and compelled me to accept the mission with all my heart, soul, mind, and strength. As I turned to look at Earth, all I could see were Adam's and Eve's face. My love for them and for all their captive children brought tears to my eyes and caused me to rise to my feet. "Let's roll." And the rescue had begun.

Leaving Heaven, being born, growing up, battling sin and temptation every day… it was the hardest thing I've ever done. A teacher of the Law once asked me what the greatest commandment was. As I searched for words to encapsulate the core meaning of life, all I could think about was what had gotten me here: "Love the Lord your God with all your heart and with all your soul and with all your mind and with all your strength and love your neighbor as yourself" (Mark 12:29-31). After all, it was this crazy deep love for my Father and for our sweet children that had driven me to leave everything, to allow myself to be beaten mercilessly, and to embrace being nailed to a cross and left there to die.

It was *your* face that I kept seeing as I fought to carry that insanely heavy cross to the top of the hill. *You* are the reason I didn't give up, didn't give in, and didn't tap out. I knew that, if I didn't complete my mission, you would still be dead and lost in your sins. My *love* for the *Father* and for *you* motivated me *every* step of the way.

What's LOVE got to do with it?

If we had to sum up Jesus' picture of motivation, we could do it with four letters: L. O. V. E. He was motivated by an insatiable love for His Father God and a burning desire to rescue you and me from the life of death we had chosen.

It might not be this high-tech, but I imagine that, behind the word *love*, His picture frame is divided into two sides. On one side, there is a picture of God, Jesus, and the Holy Spirit hanging out together before the world began. On the other, there is a slideshow of the faces of the 7.5 billion people on planet Earth. There was nothing else that drove Him. Not His financial success. Not His own fame. Not even His physical health. His singular motivation was love. It kept Him up at night. It got Him up early. It cost Him His life. But it was sufficient to carry Him all the way through.

Jesus' motivations were always completely pure and perfectly prioritized...

1. Love God with every fiber of your being.
2. Love others in the same way that you want to be loved.

What does this mean for us?

The first big takeaway is that the basis and driving factor for *anything* we *ever* do *must* be our deep love for God. Think about it. God made every sunrise and animal we see around us. He knows the hearts and hears the prayers of every single person on the face of the Earth, and He sent His only Son to rescue us from our filthy sins by dying in our place. He is the only one who has earned the right to sit on the throne of our lives, and the Bible is clear that the only way we can know how to truly love is through understanding how Jesus loved us (1 John 4:19). He came all the way to us and paid the price we deserved to pay. So when He urges us to surrender our lives to Him and to walk the path of

Jesus, our motivation should not be one of fear, because His perfect love drives out all fear; pride, because He is God and we are not; or legalism, because we can *never* earn His love (1 John 4:18; Isaiah 41; Ephesians 2:8). Our singular motivation should rather be one of deep love. "He loves me so much. Of course, I will respond in loving obedience."

The second sentence in Jesus' thesis on the meaning of life reads, "Love your neighbor as yourself." While it is *very* clear that our first, central, and most-intimate love relationship is to be with God the Father, Jesus spends every waking moment putting this love on display through loving the people God placed in His path. Again, His motivation to love both the first-century beggar and you and me was nothing other than a deep love for humanity that was birthed out of His love for God. Instead of slinking around in fear that people wouldn't like Him or puffing His chest out in pride, Jesus saw every person around Him as a reflection of His incredible Father and worthy of love. He didn't teach in the synagogue or heal the sick to keep a running tally of how holy He was. He carried out His mission because real people with real problems were real slaves to sin and death, and they needed to know the Good News.

Why do we sit with a teammate who just lost a parent to cancer? Why do we spend our lunch break fasting and praying for the particular coach God has laid on our heart? Why do we start a team Bible study so that our dearest sisters and brothers can hear the truth of the gospel? Because we have been radically loved by an unbelievable God, and we are bursting at the seams to pass it on.

No Quit in Him

Finally, I think we can draw an incredible amount of drive and gut-level motivation from just how passionate and determined Jesus was to complete His mission of love. I don't know about you, but every time the scene from *The Passion of the Christ* plays on the movie screen in my mind—where a dehydrated, broken, bloody Jesus literally wills the cross to the top of Golgotha—I can hardly keep myself from jumping to my feet and running through the nearest door, wall, or window. When I think about how tough He was and how much heart and determination He showed as He fixed His eyes on the prize—a horrible death on the cross for my sins—the "light and momentary" struggles I am facing are instantly put into perspective. Who am I to bail on a tough conversation, give into sexual temptation, or go half speed on a wind sprint when Jesus Christ—the *perfect* Son of God—*willingly* pushed Himself to the limit for me? Let's go!

There are a million different motivators on the market today, but if you want to live and move like Jesus, there is only one to choose from: love… an all-consuming, powerful love for our Creator and Savior and a deep, selfless love for everyone who crosses our path.

Glasses Check

Do you remember the glasses that I asked you to put on a while back? The ones that were securely framed in with the gospel and had lenses that were divided into four different sections? Take them off for a second, and take another look at them.

We will discuss this in further depth in the next few chapters, but just like the glasses would fall apart without the frame, you cannot exist, move, breathe, or hope to accomplish anything of eternal value without trusting in the gospel of Jesus Christ. He is your only hope for forgiveness and being made right with God. Without a deep, love relationship with the God of the Universe you will live a life of groping around in a dark room looking for a light switch. You'll never discover true peace and purpose, and you will not be able to accomplish the incredible things God created you for. However, if you believe that Jesus is who He says He is and that He died for your sins and rose again to defeat death and sin forever, you have placed your entire life and trust in the power of the gospel, and you have made God the "head coach" of your life… you are in a position to live out a life like the one Jesus did when He walked the earth.

God's *goal* for our lives is clear: that we would become more like His Son Jesus. Whatever we do and wherever we are, we should not stop until we look, talk, move, smell, sound, and love just like Jesus. We should realize that God will not stop using every situation to shape us.

In God's arena, *winning* has nothing to do with the electronic scoreboard and everything to do with the scoreboard of your heart. Did you take every last ounce of strength and ability that God gave you and "put it in the game" toward the goal of becoming more like Jesus? If so, you are winner… no matter what the numbers say.

We always compete for an *audience*. God desires to be our only audience. At the end of the day, we live, move, and compete to please only Him, our true head coach.

Finally, there are so many *motivations* to choose from, but the only one that will allow us to reach our goal, to win consistently, and to please our Heavenly audience of one is true love.

Do you believe that?

If so, pop those fancy glasses back on, make sure your tray table is in an upright and locked position, and hold on for the final leg of the ride!

TRAINING TIME

1. What is your primary motivation in the arena of competition? What drives you? Why do you do what you do?
2. How does it make you feel to know that Jesus' motivation to embrace the cross was His deep love for you?
3. What would it look like for you to be motivated by a deep love for God and for the people around you?
4. What application of the truths of this chapter do you want to make in your life?

14

PARADISE LOST

For although they knew God, they neither glorified him as
God nor gave thanks to him, but their thinking became futile
and their foolish hearts were darkened... they exchanged the
truth of God for a lie, and worshiped and served created things
rather than the Creator.

—ROMANS 1:21-23, 25

As for you, you were dead in your transgressions and sins, in
which you used to live when you followed the ways of this
world and of the ruler of the kingdom of the air, the spirit who
is now at work in those who are disobedient.

—EPHESIANS 2:1-2

BRIAN JONES WAS A 15-YEAR-OLD BASKETBALL PHENOM. As a freshman, he had averaged more points per game, more steals, and more assists than any other player in the conference. He was lightning quick, a natural-born leader, and an unstoppable force on the court. In addition to being one of the hottest up-and-coming young players in the state, Brian was a great kid. His father was the pastor of a local church, and he had the incredible good fortune of growing up in a home where his parents were happily married and where he knew he was loved. After every game, win or lose, his dad would make a beeline for him, give him a big bear hug, and tell him how proud he was of him and how much he loved him. As often as they could, while his mom would take his younger sister home, Brian and his dad would pile into his old truck and drive to the place that meant the most to them, the top of the bluff right outside of town. There, under the stars, they would talk about life, basketball, God, and what it meant to be a man... until they would finish their chocolate milkshakes and figure it was time to head home and finish the day's homework. Brian's father was always quick to remind his son that God loved him and had incredible, amazing things planned for him, and Brian simply loved getting to spend time with his dad.

Slow Fade

At the beginning of his sophomore season, however, things began to change. After the first game of the season, while Brian was on his way to the locker room to get cleaned up before joining his dad for a celebratory chocolate milkshake, Erika—one of the senior cheerleaders—ran up to him and told him what a great game he had played. Eager to get to the bluff, Brian said, "Uh, thanks," and he started toward the locker room.

But before he could get moving, she grabbed him and, with a wink, said, "By the way, I'm your biggest fan..."

As she turned and walked back to the group of cheerleaders, Brian could feel his heart racing as he tried to make sense of what had just happened.

The milkshake that night was accompanied by talk about how important it was to be a man who truly loved God on and off the court, and how one of the ways Brian could show God that he loved and trusted Him was to honor Him with his body and to fight like crazy to save himself sexually for his wife. Brian and his father had often talked about this topic of sexual purity and respecting the young women in his life. But tonight, for some reason, all Brian could do was nod silently while his mind replayed Erika's comments over and over again like a scratched CD.

The next chapter of the story reads like any other tragedy. Before long, his father's postgame bear hugs were replaced by Brian racing to the sideline to get a victory kiss from his girlfriend, Erika. The victory milkshakes and heart-to-hearts also became less and less frequent as

Brian would choose instead to follow Erika to the late-night parties to which she had introduced him. Before long, the deep intimacy between Brian and his father had been replaced with a cold, standoffishness. Brian wasn't sure if his Dad knew that he had been sleeping with Erika for the past couple of months, but he knew he had to do everything in his power to hide this new part of his life from him. He was certain that, if his dad found out, he would be so angry and disappointed that things would never be the same.

Reality Strikes

One Monday morning at school, Brian couldn't find Erika anywhere. Just as he was about to get worried, he got a text from her that said, "Call me." He slipped out the back door of the school and holed up in the corner of the baseball dugout where no one could see him and then dialed her number. When she answered, he could tell she was upset, and when he asked what was wrong, she blurted out, "I found out three weeks ago that I was pregnant, and I went this morning to put an end to it." Before she could even finish, Brian dropped the phone and started sprinting toward his car. He couldn't believe it. Just six months before, he had been staring up at the stars, enjoying his father's love and drinking in his wisdom about life. And now, he had not only lost the most precious relationship in his life, he had given himself away sexually and now, as a result of his choices, had cost his own baby its life. As he slammed his car into gear and peeled out of the parking lot, all he could think about was how he had ruined his life and that he had to get as far away from home as possible.

By the time Brian's dad arrived at the basketball game, the stands were already buzzing with speculation as to where their star player was. No one could find him anywhere. When they called his phone, it just rang and rang. As soon as he heard that his son was missing, Brian's father jumped into action, calling every person he knew and driving around town in a desperate search for his boy.

Finally, a dispatcher from the sheriff's department returned a call saying that a vehicle matching the description of Brian's had been spotted two counties over. The car was totaled. Brian was safe, but he was being held in the county jail on charges of speeding and reckless endangerment.

Time Out

Before we go any further down the path of this young man's destruction, we need to realize that Brian's story is actually *our* story.

In the beginning, God created the earth and everything in it. And it was good… really, really good. I'm talking about no rainy days. No thorns on roses. Bananas the size of your arm good! Oh, yeah! Once our incredible planet was finished, God "created man in His own image" (Genesis 1:27) and placed him in the biggest, most amazing garden you have ever seen "to work it and take care of it" (Genesis 2:15). God gave man free reign over everything that He had created, even charging him with the task of ruling over all of the living creatures on earth. He trusted him, believed in him, and endowed his life with an incredible purpose. The only rule God put in place was very clear: Adam and his new wife, Eve, weren't allowed to eat from the tree in the middle of the garden (the one that gave the knowledge of good and evil). And the consequence was pretty clear, too: if "you eat of it, you will surely die" (Genesis 2:17). Simple. Right? Come, live in this awesome garden, hangout with God all day long, and be fulfilled in the work of taking care of all of creation; just don't eat from one, tiny tree. Party on!

You and I were created to be in an intimate, beautiful, meaningful, awesome relationship with the God of the Universe. He made every human being on the planet (all 7.5 billion of us) with the desire to sit in the back of an old pickup truck with us to look up at the stars, drink a chocolate milkshake, and talk about everything under the sun. The only reason you and I are here on planet Earth breathing oxygen right now is because we were created to find unbelievable peace and fulfillment in knowing Him, loving Him, and serving Him with our lives… period.

Unfortunately, like we briefly examined before, the story doesn't end there. It's pretty obvious that we are a long way from walking with God in a beautiful garden paradise where there is no cancer, theft, murder, or suicide. So, what in the world happened?

Just like Brian, man was tempted to believe a lie. In the third chapter of the first book of the Bible, God's bitter enemy, Satan, showed up in the form of a snake to tempt God's precious children to walk down the path of death. Like he always does, Satan lied and twisted God's words to plant a seed of doubt in Eve's mind, one that I'm sure was as persistent as a mosquito on a humid summer night. Soon, Adam and Eve had both swallowed the enemy's lie that God had been holding out on them and that they would be better off if they just ate the fruit—which was extremely good-looking and tasty, by the way (Genesis 3:6).

Missing the Mark

For the sake of definition, what Adam and Eve did is called *sin*. Sin is simply when we miss the mark of God's perfection. It can come either by directly choosing to do something we know is against God's character, by slipping and falling into something that we weren't careful or thoughtful enough to avoid, or by ignoring the good we know God wants us to do. Any way you slice it, sin is looking God in the face and telling Him you don't care about Him, that you know what you need better than He does, and that you want what you want when you want it. Sin stinks. It is gross, destructive, and if left unchecked, can grow from a slightly embarrassing and annoying seed into an enormous tree that leads to the death of your hopes, dreams, joy, future, and eventually *you*. Not only can sin crush you, total your car, and leave you in a county jail, it can also destroy your relationship with the people around you and, most importantly, your relationship with your Heavenly Father. You see, God is so holy and perfect that even one sin—one teeny, tiny, seemingly insignificant sin—makes it impossible to have a relationship with your Heavenly Father. He never changes. And while He stands there with open arms and more love for us than we could ever imagine, we are busy stacking up brick after brick between us and Him when we choose to indulge our lust, greed, selfishness, pride, insecurity, or anger (just to name a few). Just like Adam and Eve, *you and I* have willfully, intentionally, and repeatedly looked God in the face and decided to choose sin over Him. We are *all* sinners, all 7.5 billion of us.

A High Cost

Brian's sin cost him, his school, his girlfriend, his family, and his unborn child tremendously. Your sins may have cost you more than that. I can look back on my life and see very clear consequences for my selfish, sinful choices. But the greatest consequence of all was given to our first sinful ancestors, Adam and Eve. God was clear that, if they disobeyed Him and ate from the tree, they would die. Indeed, they did die some years later after living out a difficult life full of painful and unfulfilling work, frustrating relationship issues, and enduring the heartache of watching one of their sons murder his brother in a jealous rage. These hardships, however, don't even hold a candle to the greatest consequence of their sin… their fractured relationship with their Creator and Heavenly Father.

Once Adam and Eve sinned, their relationship with God was mortally wounded. The earliest evidence of the broken fellowship was their attempt to run away from their poor decision and to hide from God and each other in the bushes. Once God found them and explained to them the consequences of their rebellion, He ushered Adam and Eve out of the beautiful garden and locked the gate behind them. In my opinion, even worse than having to leave their beautiful garden home, their greatest loss at that moment was that of their ability literally to walk with, talk with, and enjoy perfect, awesome fellowship with their Creator God. They gave up *everything* for a stupid piece of fruit and the ability to make a selfish decision.

The rest of the first half of the Bible reads a lot like Brian's story: a heartbroken, love-sick Father does everything in His power to bring His child home… while His wayward child speeds away from Him on a selfish, destructive path filled with sadness, loss, and death. As God's story continues to unfold, two things are very clear: 1) He has not stopped pursuing the hearts of the people He created and 2) all humans are born absolute slaves to a self-absorbed life of sin that keeps them lost, lonely, bitter, and a long way from God's embrace. This is my reality. This is your reality. And if God hadn't launched the greatest and most improbable rescue mission of all time, we would be doomed to live and die in this reality for all eternity, and we would never have the opportunity to be an eternal competitor. But fortunately for us and for Brian, our story doesn't end here.

__TRAINING TIME__

1. What is the most difficult part of Brian's story for you? Why?
2. How does knowing that you were "created to be in an intimate, beautiful, meaningful, awesome relationship with the God of the Universe" change your view of yourself?
3. Where do you see yourself (and your sin) in the stories about Isaiah, Adam, and Eve?
4. What application of the truths of this chapter do you want to make in your life?

15

RECKLESS LOVE

There is no difference, for all have sinned and fall short of the glory of God, and are justified freely by his grace through the redemption that came by Christ Jesus.

—ROMANS 3:22-24

But while he was still a long way off, his father saw him and was filled with compassion for him; he ran to his son, threw his arms around him and kissed him.

—LUKE 15:20

IT DIDN'T TAKE HIM LONG. After Brian's father received the call from the sheriff's department, it was only a matter of a half hour or so before he pulled into a parking space at the county jail. The basketball game was the farthest thing from his mind as he drove the backroads of his son's destructive path just a few hours earlier. "How did my boy end up here?" he wondered aloud to God. He wasn't blind; he had seen the changes in his son. But like any good father, he knew he couldn't force his son to love him. He knew his son would have to make his own choice either to follow the narrow, difficult path of life or the wide, smooth path of destruction. But he never thought it would go this far.

As Brian's father talked with the officer on duty, he was faced with the stark reality that Brian met hours earlier: this was no joke. Brian had broken the law, and he would either pay the penalty of his crime immediately or spend the rest of his life locked in a tiny room until he did. Fortunately for Brian, because he was a minor, there was a provision in the state's law that made it possible for him to plead guilty to the charges, pay the penalty on the spot, and be back with his family that evening. Unfortunately, the $23 Brian had in his wallet wasn't nearly enough to cover the $5,000 fine for which he would be liable. On top of that, his car was now totaled, so he had no way to get anywhere. To make matters even worse, the thought of seeing the hurt in his father's eyes made him want to find a new place to live… forever.

Brian's mind was flooded with guilt and pain. *How did I get here?* he wondered. Everything he had worked for was gone, and he was stuck in a God-forsaken jail cell miles away from anyone he knew and loved. It was so dark and hopeless that, for a moment, he scanned the cell for a way to escape the anguish by putting an end to all of it… by putting an end to himself. But when that search proved fruitless, he simply slumped into the corner and cried.

One Call

After a while, he came to his senses and remembered he had seen on TV that every prisoner gets one phone call. His mind raced as he thought about how best to use his one shot at calling for help. He thought of calling Erika, but for the first time, he saw what his life had become because of his choice to follow her. He realized how far he had wandered from everything he held dear. He saw how he had willingly chosen to embrace the lifestyle of death that went along with his relationship with her. The sorrow he felt because of his choices and of the pain he had put his father through overwhelmed him, and he was again reduced to a sobbing heap in the corner of his cell.

He had tried to be a man, but now more than ever, he realized he was just a little boy who was alone, lost, scared, and in need of his daddy. The choice was clear. He had to call the one who had loved him and fought for him throughout his life. He had to call his father.

Brian stood up, and as he looked for a way to get his hands on a phone, he was confused by what he saw through the bars of his cell. The door at the end of the hall opened, and his father burst through, followed by one of the guards. Brian watched as his father's eyes desperately darted from cell to cell until they came to rest on his son. Disregarding anyone else in the room, his father dropped the papers he was holding and sprinted toward his son.

Brian blurted out, "Dad! I am so sorry! I have screwed everything up! I've hurt God, and I've hurt you. And now, I'm stuck in here. I wanna come home. I wanna come back to you and to God. And I promise I will spend my whole life making it up to you! I just…"

As if by magic, the cell door opened, the guard removed Brian's chains, and his father put him in a bear hug that was so tight he couldn't breathe.

The Exchange

As they drove home along the roads that had landed him in jail, Brian sat in silence, not sure what had just happened and not sure of what the future would hold.

His father spoke first. "Son, do realize what happened today?"

Still not exactly sure what had happened, Brian just turned his head and looked at his father.

"Son, today was a culmination of a series of poor choices… selfish choices… and what you experienced was what happens when you choose death over life and sin over God's best for you."

Brian knew his father was right. The previous few months had been terrible. He could now vividly see how each poor decision had built upon the previous one to take him to a place he never intended to go.

His father continued. "I spoke with Erika's parents this afternoon, and I know all about…" his voice broke up. "I know all about… your child…" He was visibly crying now. "Son… I am so sorry. It was never meant to be this way."

Brian couldn't believe it. His dad knew all about his sexual relationship with Erika and the horrible consequences of his reckless behavior! He thought for sure that, if his dad ever found out about any of that, he would be cast out of the family forever.

Again, his father spoke. "Son, you have no idea how much I love you and how desperately your mother and I have been praying for you ever since we started noticing you were slipping away. Do you even know why you are sitting here with me and not still bound up like an animal in that cell?"

Brian racked his brain. He hadn't been able to put the pieces together to make sense of why they had let him go. *Maybe Dad posted bail? Maybe I'll have to go to court and face my punishment there? Maybe Dad paid the fine and I'll have to work like a dog for years to pay him back?* He wasn't sure. Either way, Brian knew he owed somebody something. He'd seen enough movies to know that you don't just walk free without paying the penalty for your mistakes. *Maybe...*

His father's gentle hand on his shoulder cut off his stream of thought. "Son, you're free right now because *I* paid your penalty. I spoke with the officer on duty. He called the judge, and we worked out a deal. Son, they allowed me to pay the penalty for your speeding and reckless endangerment as if I was the one who had been driving. I paid the $5,000 fine. I will serve the hours of community service. And, come tomorrow, I will be the one with the revoked driver's license and the stain on my criminal record."

"No!" Brian screamed. "You're lying! It can't be like that! I was the one who was an idiot! I was the one who made the stupid, selfish decisions. And I was the one who smashed the car! I won't let you do it, Dad! No! You can't! Take me back to the jail. I've got to handle this on my own. You can't ruin your life for me!"

"Son, it's too late. It is finished. There's nothing you can do to change what I've done for you. I knew exactly what I was doing, and it was my choice to do this on your behalf. It was the only way to show you how much I truly love you and that my love isn't based on whether or not you make the right choices. If it had gone any other way, you'd always wonder in the back of your mind if I was secretly still mad at you. So, as it stands, the debt has been paid. You don't owe me a thing. You are free. Son, you know how I feel about you. Now, you have to decide what you're going to do about it."

For what seemed like the tenth time that day, Brian's head was spinning. Why would his dad do that? How could he have known everything Brian had done... every selfish decision... and still chosen to love him this way? Was this for real?

Life or Death

He was certain about one thing. His dad was right about the crossroads at which Brian found himself. He had to make a choice. He could take his newfound freedom, tell his dad to get lost, and jump back into the mix with Erika and her crew. Or, he could embrace the second chance afforded to him by his father's love and spend the rest of his days getting to know him again, learning what it looks like to live a life that expresses the same kind of love that was shown to him. The choice was simple. Brian knew there was no way he could trade the deep love of his father for the fleeting pursuit of the pleasures of this life. He had to humble himself and embrace the reality that his father's love had set him free. On top of all that, he was now keenly aware of how deeply he missed the chocolate milkshakes and long heart-to-heart chats on the bluff that had so shaped his heart. He wanted to come home again... for good. And he knew there was no sense in delaying the choice that was burning in his heart.

"Dad, I know I blew it. I'm so sorry. I don't even know how to say thank you for taking my punishment. It's unbelievable. Thank you. I can't imagine how hard it was for you and Mom to watch me choose the path I've been on for the past couple of months. Man, I never want to go back there again, and if you'll have me back, I would love to come home and be your son again. I'm dying to go back to the way things used to be when we were so close and everything was so good. I'm not perfect, and I don't even know what it looks like to dig my way out of where I am, but I know I can't do it alone. I'm gonna need your help, Dad. But I'm all in for as long as it takes... no matter what. Will you help me?"

TRAINING TIME

1. Describe a time when your poor choices had you trapped like Brian? How did you get out?
2. Has anyone ever loved you the way Brian's father loved him? If so, how did it make you feel?
3. How would you respond to the free gift of a second chance? Why?
4. What application of the truths of this chapter do you want to make in your life?

16

THE RESCUE

*Once you were alienated from God and were enemies in your
minds because of your evil behavior. But now he has reconciled
you by Christ's physical body through death to present you holy
in his sight, without blemish and free from accusation – if you
continue in your faith, established and firm, not moved from
the hope held out in the gospel.*

—COLOSSIANS 1:21-23

*I tell you the truth, everyone who sins is a slave to sin. Now a
slave has no permanent place in the family, but a son belongs
to it forever. So if the Son sets you free, you will be free indeed!*

—JOHN 8:34-36

THINK ABOUT WHAT BRIAN'S FATHER DID. Watch closely because
this is the part of the story where all the threads begin to come together
to weave the incredible tapestry of the gospel, God's "good news" for all
of humanity, that is running behind, through, and as the foundation of
the *true, eternal* reality that God longs to open our eyes to.

You see, Brian's father could have stayed in the stands at the basketball game. He had every right to be fed up with his son's behavior.
The destruction of their relationship was nobody's fault but Brian's. I'll
even bet that, if he had taken a poll of the parents at the game, he could
have found at least a handful of folks who would have said, "Let your
son figure it out on his own. He made the poor decisions... not you. It's
up to him to figure his own way out of the mess he made." And they

would have been right! No one deserved to pay for Brian's mistakes but him.

No one deserves to pay for our sin but us... period. Brian was guilty. We are guilty. If you have ever lied, stolen *anything*, or looked at someone with lust or anger in your heart (the list goes on), you are guilty of breaking God's law and are criminally responsible for paying the penalty of your sin. The penalties for his actions were a fine of $5,000, community service, and a revoked license. The penalty for our sin is much heavier. The penalty for our sin is a broken relationship with our Heavenly Father and eternal death.

You see, God could have stayed in the stands, too. He had every right to be fed up with the selfish, sinful, murderous, adulterous, and hateful ways of the people He created. Every single person on Earth had turned their back on Him at one time or another, and He would have been completely justified to sit back and watch us destroy ourselves and the planet He created. He did not *have* to do anything, but like any good father, His desperate love for His children forced Him to act. As He watched you, me, and all of humanity slowly suffocating to death in our lives of hollow, fleeting, selfish pursuits, His love for us would not allow Him to look away. With His own heart wrapped up in our lives and pain, He devised a plan to defeat sin once and for all and to create a way for us to walk freely with Him again.

The Rescue

As we begin to unpack the details of God's rescue mission, we come to learn some pretty amazing things about Jesus. One of the most incredible and important things about Jesus is that—unlike you, me, and everyone else who has ever breathed Earth's oxygen—Jesus never sinned (2 Corinthians 5:21). The Bible says that He faced every type of temptation that we all face but that He walked through it without choosing sin over God... not even once!

Because of His spotless sin record, Jesus was blameless in God's eyes. There were no sin barriers between Him and His holy and perfect Father, so they enjoyed an incredible relationship as a result. As we look at the stories of Jesus' life in the Bible, the evidence of His relationship with God is everywhere. He talked to His Father about everything, often sneaking out early in the morning or staying up super late simply to spend time talking with Him. Jesus loved His Father and delighted in obeying Him, only saying the words, doing the deeds, and going to the places His Father asked of Him. In addition to knowing and loving God, Jesus poured every ounce of His strength, determination, and creativity into serving His Father with His life, even when it was uncomfortable or difficult to do so.

Are you starting to see the plan unfold?

We cry out from the darkness, being hopelessly trapped in our sins. Motivated by His outrageous love for His children, God devised a plan to send His Son Jesus to Earth to be born and to live as one of us. Out of obedience to His Father, Jesus left Heaven and lived a blameless life on Earth as a secret agent on a mission to ransom us back from darkness and death.

The Greatest Mission

After three years of His ministry, the religious leaders of the day decided they'd had enough of Jesus. His persistent claims that He was the Son of God and His obnoxious yet miraculous ability to heal people was causing division among their followers and making their lives difficult. So, like God's enemies have been doing since the beginning of the world (and still continue to do today), they devised a plan to shut Jesus up and regain power. They decided to kill Him.

It happened easily enough. They enticed one of His followers to betray Jesus by offering money to him. And once Jesus was on trial, they stirred up the crowd against Him, and He was given the death penalty. After living a selfless life for 33 years, God's sinless Son stood before the people He had come to save, chained as a criminal and condemned to die.

Can you imagine how Jesus must have felt? Maybe you can. Maybe you know all too well how it feels to be hurting and humiliated in public. But a beautiful thing about the story of God's gospel and how Jesus came to save us is that He knows *exactly* what we are going through because He has been there. He didn't live a sheltered existence away from the hurts of the world. Rather, He dove headfirst into the very brokenness that held God's beloved children captive. No matter what you are going through, He knows, and He didn't give up. Despite the pain and the shame, He took every step with you and me on His mind, knowing He had to make it. Quitting and failing His mission was not an option. The cost was far too high.

God could have saved the world from sin by sending Jesus to say,

> I was just kidding about the whole sin thing. It's not really that big of a deal. Just keep living life the way you want to, and I'll change the rules to make sure there are no consequences for your sin so we can be cool again.

But, He didn't. His justice and the death penalty for sin were unflinching, and Jesus knew it. In case you are tempted to feel bad for Jesus as though His Father double-crossed Him or something, the Bible is clear that Jesus accepted the mission, knowing full well that He was coming to Earth to die. And when we look at a handful of places in the first half of the Bible, it's clear that Jesus knew exactly how He was going to die. Yet, He chose to come anyway… to rescue you and me.

More Than It Seems

From the outside, God's rescue plan looked like an epic failure. Instead of coming on the scene with the military power and political might necessary to free the Jewish people from the evil Romans, here was Jesus— the teacher and healer who claimed to be God's Son and promised "good news for the poor, freedom for the prisoners, recovery of sight for the blind and release for the oppressed"—hanging naked, lifeless, and alone on a piece of wood outside of the city… for us. To the casual passerby, it seemed that Jesus was nothing but a phony, a conceited liar who stirred up trouble and got what He deserved. But because the invisible and eternal undercurrent of the gospel that has been weaving its way through

God's entire story, we know Jesus' death was necessary. It was the only way God could rescue us, once and for all, from the penalty of our sins and bring us back into the perfect relationship with Himself we were designed to enjoy.

It's not meant to be complicated.

We are broken, sinful people who have turned our backs on God and wandered a long way from home. We are stuck in a jail cell a million miles from the embrace of our Heavenly Father with a death sentence hanging over our heads. The only way out is to pay the penalty. But if we elect to pay it ourselves, we'll end up dead, still separated from God in a lonely, dark place of eternal torment that the Bible calls *Hell* that is set aside for sinners and enemies of God. However, the good news of the gospel is that God's Son Jesus shed His blood to pay for the sins of the whole world. Think about it… 2,000 years ago, Jesus died on a cross to pay for the sins of all of humanity by satisfying the death penalty that held us captive. He died for *everyone's* sins. Osama bin Laden's. Hitler's. Saddam Hussein's. The guys' who nailed Him to the cross. Yours. Mine. All of ours. Every sin you have ever committed or will ever commit—even the biggest, grossest, darkest ones that nobody knows about—has been paid for by Jesus. Because of what He did on the cross, you have the chance to accept His payment for your sin and to sprint out of your prison cell and into the loving arms of your Heavenly Father today. It's paid for. You don't deserve it. You can't do anything to pay it back. It is finished.

What are you going to do about it?

TRAINING TIME

1. Why do you think sin is such a big deal to God? Why couldn't He just let us off the hook?
2. How does knowing the high price that Jesus paid change the way you view your sin?
3. How does it make you feel to know that all your sins have been paid for?

4. What application of the truths of this chapter do you want to make in your life?

17

THE ENCORE

Praise be to the God and Father of our Lord Jesus Christ! In his great mercy he has given us new birth into a living hope through the resurrection of Jesus Christ from the dead.

—1 PETER 1:3

Here I am! I stand at the door and knock. If anyone hears my voice and opens the door, I will come in and eat with him, and he with me.

—REVELATION 3:20

DO YOU REMEMBER THE FINAL SCENE of the movie *Cinderella Man?* I'll set the stage for you.

In a riveting true story, underdog boxer James Braddock has just gone the distance against the defending world champion Max Baer. It was a spectacular fight in which both men landed some heavy punches, but the final bell has sounded, and the winner will be decided by the flurry of judges outside the ring.

The tension in Madison Square Garden could be cut with a knife. Max Baer parades around the ring in a show of false confidence, hoping with every fiber in his being that the victory will be his. James Braddock humbly shrugs as his manager tends to a cut above his eye, just happy to be standing after 12 rounds. The pro-Braddock crowd shifts nervously in their seats as the radio announcer says, "I'll tell you this much... If they take this long to make a decision, they're gonna decide to screw somebody."

The heavy breathing of the fighters is the only sound heard as the head referee approaches the microphone with the verdict. "Ladies and Gentlemen, we have your decision. It's unanimous! Winner... and the new world heavyweight champion... James J. Braddock!" As the crowd explodes, Braddock is lifted into the air, and the camera drifts up into the rafters, leaving you with a bird's-eye view of the victory celebration that your heart longed for but that your brain told you was impossible. Everything you believed about and hoped for your hero as you watched his life march toward this climactic moment was validated by the shrill voice of the radio announcer saying, "James Braddock has defeated Max Baer for the heavyweight championship of the world!"

The Greatest Victory

When the final bell of Jesus' life rang, it didn't look good, either. He was broken and bloody, and His opponent Satan was dancing around the ring, gloating in victory. As Jesus' body was taken down from the cross and placed in a tomb, His followers had to face the apparent reality of the situation: Jesus was dead. Their hearts were torn because they had truly believed that Jesus was God's Son and that He was going to usher in God's eternal Kingdom as their victorious savior. They had clearly heard Jesus say He would have to die but that God would raise Him back to life after three days. Nevertheless, their current state of shock and grief kept them from putting the pieces together. So they sat in stunned silence as they tried desperately to make sense of their lives in light of what had just happened.

While God was deeply grieved by the death of His Son, He knew that the story couldn't have gone any other way if it was to capture the hearts and minds of *all* of His children. God knew that the only way to pay for the sins of the world was for Jesus to die and that the only way to set His children free forever was for Jesus to conquer sin and death by rising from the grave.

On the third day after His brutal beating and execution, two of Jesus' closest followers went to visit His grave. As the women came over the final hill, they couldn't believe their eyes. The massive stone that the soldiers had rolled in front of the opening of the tomb was sitting awkwardly off to the side, leaving the passageway into the tomb exposed. They began to run toward the tomb. As they pushed their way through the narrow rock opening, they were again astounded by what they saw. Instead of the stiff corpse they had laid to rest days earlier on the cold rock slab, the women saw two angels sitting on the ledge and only the sheet with which they had wrapped Jesus' body. As the women fell to the ground in sheer terror, one of the angels looked at them and said,

> "Why do you look for the living among the dead? He is not here; he has risen! Remember how he told you, while he was still with you in Galilee: 'The Son of Man must be delivered into the hands of sinners, be crucified and on the third day be raised again.'" (Luke 24:5-7)

At that moment, with their faces pressed to the floor of the empty tomb, they remembered all of the times when Jesus tried to tell them that this was going to happen. They had always been confused about what He meant. They knew Jesus was special, and they even believed He was God's Son, but they had never been able to wrap their brains around the fact that He would literally die and come back to life. But here they were in the very place they had laid their dead leader, face to face with the reality that He had been telling them the truth and that His plan had worked! They scrambled to their feet and sprinted as fast as they could back to the place where the rest of Jesus' friends were staying to tell them what they had seen.

Cinderella Man would have been a good story even if we had never found out that Braddock won the title. It would have been fascinating and perhaps even inspiring only to watch him go toe to toe with Max Baer like he did. But knowing that, on March 22, 1935 in Madison Square Garden, American boxer of Irish descent James J. Braddock defied all odds to *win* the world heavyweight title brings a whole new level of power and wholeness to his story. The same holds true for Jesus' story. To know that He lived and died is good. But to know that the grave couldn't hold Him down and that He defeated sin and death forever through His resurrection completes the beautiful story of God's gospel, His good news for all of humanity.

What does it all mean?

It's so simple. Jesus came to take away your sins so you could be reconciled with your Heavenly Father... right where you are sitting... right now. God loves you and longs to walk with you, to lead you, to speak with you, and to comfort and empower you through His Holy Spirit for the rest of your days on Earth... and for all eternity.

Like we dove into before, an incredible picture of our reality is this: God wants a relationship with you. In the final book of the Bible, Jesus says,

> Here I am! I stand at the door and knock. If anyone hears my voice and opens the door, I will come in and eat with him, and he with me. (Revelation 3:20)

This is not the language of a vengeful, angry God who is waiting to strike you down when you step out of line. These are the words of someone who has looked up your address, bought flowers for you, and has put His heart on the line by ringing your doorbell... knowing full well that so many will leave Him on the front porch while they scurry around inside their empty homes with the door securely bolted shut. God's not looking for those whose houses are swept clean and in order, nor is He looking for those who are perfect. (He already knows that only His Son Jesus was perfect.) Rather, He is pursuing each of us, hoping against hope that all of His children will trust Jesus' payment for their sins, open the door to their hearts, and spend the rest of their days getting to know Him, learning to love Him, and working with all their might to serve Him.

Once you say "yes" to God's proposal of an exclusive, life-giving relationship, you are a new creation. The old is gone, and a new life of purpose and wholeness has come. The weight of the thousands of sins you have been carrying is lifted and replaced with the deep reality that you are now a part of God's beloved family. Nothing you do will ever make God love you any more or any less than He does right now.

Not only are you adopted as His own, the coolest thing happens; He actually takes up residence *inside* of you through His Holy Spirit. In addition to counseling, comforting, and strengthening you, this Spirit is given as a symbol (like a wedding ring), marking you as His own. As you begin to walk as Jesus did, the Holy Spirit will open your eyes to the hidden and eternal nature of life and competition. He will break your heart for the brokenness that is hiding just below the surface of the world around you. And He will give special gifts and abilities to you so you can be His hands and feet to bring the gospel of His grace to the people who are desperate for it.

From professional athletes to little league baseball coaches... from crack addicts to the nicest guys on the block... we all have the same questions to answer:

- "Do I *know* God?"
- "What do I believe about Jesus?"
- "How am I responding to the gospel?"

No one else can answer these questions for you. They are ones that require each of us to take a long, deep look inside of ourselves to draw out the answers. While it may be difficult to see the truth through all of the hurt you carry and lies you have believed, I beg you to set this book down for five minutes, close your eyes, and search the most intimate parts of your soul for *your* answers to these questions. Everything we have talked about and everything we will journey through for the rest of our days hinges on the deep reality of God's gospel that weaves its truth through every experience we will ever have. So, please, take five minutes to examine yourself. I'll be right here waiting...

***

Most likely, when you are honest with yourself about your answers to these questions, you'll generally end up in one of four places.

1: You know God.

You have trusted Jesus as your Savior. You are leaning on and living out God's gospel daily. You are not perfect, but you are fighting with all your might to walk like Jesus as you seek to know, love, and serve God more deeply.

Praise God! Continue to walk the walk and talk the talk. Hold on tightly to His hand and enjoy the ride. When you fall down, get back up and remain on the lookout for how He might want you to be His hands and feet in any given situation.

2: You have trusted Jesus as your Savior at some point in the past, but you are not currently walking with God.

You feel like you have a pretty good grasp on the gospel, but it doesn't affect your daily life. You know some things about God, but your life is more characterized by sin than by a deep, intimate relationship with your Heavenly Father. To put it bluntly, you said "yes" to God's marriage proposal, but you have been cheating on Him with everyone and everything that makes you feel good. You know there is something better than where you are right now. You want to leave your life of sin. You're tired, lonely, and miserable. You want to go back home, but you don't have any idea how God would react if you showed up in His driveway.

Come home! God has been scanning the horizon ever since you wandered away, longing to see your silhouette pop up over the ridge so He could run to you, embrace you, put His robe on your shoulders, put His ring on your finger, and throw an unbelievable party to celebrate your homecoming back from a faraway land. This will not be easy. It will require a ton of honesty with God, yourself, and others, but His Holy Spirit will give you everything you need while constantly reminding you that you are His beloved child. I pray that my story will serve as an encouragement for you as you readjust to life in the Father's house. Welcome home!

3: You've never met God.

You know some things about Jesus, but you have never trusted Him as your Savior. You may have heard the gospel before, but you've never listened… until now. Your life has been characterized by selfish, empty pursuits. You have lived solely for your own pleasure, and it didn't matter who you had to run over or what you had to do to get what you wanted. There are parts of your past that you haven't shared with anyone, and you have sins and addictions that you thought would be with you forever. You are tired, empty, and fed up with chasing the things that the world calls valuable. You want a new life. You want to be rid of your sins. You desperately want a true relationship with the God who created you. You believe Jesus died for your sins, and you are ready to trust Him as your Savior. You want to say "yes" to God's proposal and to spend the rest of your life learning to know, love, and serve Him.

Surrender! Open the door, throw up your hands, and offer all that you have (good, bad, ugly) to God. Tell Him about the ways you have fallen short and chosen your own pleasure over Him. Tell Him you are sorry. With all your heart, tell Him you believe that Jesus died to pay for your sins and rose again to defeat sin and death forever. Ask Him for His help as you learn what it means to live as His child. Ask Him to teach you how to know, love, and serve Him with every fiber of your being.

Find somebody who you know loves God, tell that person about the decision you made, and ask him or her to teach you about this new life. Find a group of other Jesus followers to support, challenge, and encourage you.

Read your Bible every day. You don't have to read a billion chapters a day. Start with one each day, and watch God transform you through His living Word.

Finally, talk to God as often and as honestly as you want. He desires to be a part of every ounce of your life. I pray that my story will be a picture that helps you as you begin your new life with God. Welcome to the family!

4: You are running from God.

Maybe you've kept the door of your heart firmly locked as Jesus has been knocking. You've heard the gospel, but you have chosen to live by a different set of beliefs, hoping they will pay off in the end. You are not ready to believe or trust in Jesus, and you may not even see the need for a savior. *You* are the supreme guiding force of your life, and you are doing the best you know how to navigate through this fragile and broken world.

God loves you. He desires you. But He will not kick down the door to your heart. You must open it on your own. Because I love you, I must tell you that you are choosing to live in a very difficult and dangerous place. You are choosing an existence, for both now and eternity, apart from the presence of your loving Creator. I stand firmly with the Bible when it states, "He who has the Son has life; he who does not have the Son of God does not have life" (1 John 5:12). It is my deepest and most sincere prayer that you would hear Him calling your name and respond. I pray that the story He has written through my life will reveal His face to you.

***

Wherever you land and however you answer these questions of the heart, my hope is that my story and few chapters will help you to understand how deeply God loves you and that He is willing to go to any lengths possible to invite you into His great story.

__TRAINING TIME__

1. How does the fact that Jesus is alive separate Christianity from all other world religions?
2. At this point in the story, on a scale of 1 to 10, how confident are you in your understanding of the basic points of the gospel (good news) of Jesus? What questions do you still have?

3. With regard to the gospel, which of the four groups do you believe you fall into? What do you feel called to do today in response to the truth of the gospel?
4. What application of the truths of this chapter do you want to make in your life?

18

GAME TIME

Everyone then who hears these words of mine and does them will be like a wise man who built his house on the rock.

—MATTHEW 7:24

I call heaven and earth to witness against you today, that I have set before you life and death, blessing and curse. Therefore choose life, that you and your offspring may live, loving the LORD your God, obeying his voice and holding fast to him, for he is your life and length of days, that you may dwell in the land that the LORD swore to your fathers.

—DEUTERONOMY 30:19-20

I DON'T KNOW EXACTLY HOW LONG THE MOMENT REALLY LASTS, but there is no denying that it's there. It's that moment right before the puck drops, the first pitch is thrown, or the ball explodes off the first tee. In this moment as your eyes focus, your heart races, and every hair stands on end, you have a decision to make. Will you fight, or will you run? Will you embrace the challenge, or will you shrink from it? Will you get in the game, or will you get back on the bus? I think this moment is exactly where we find ourselves right now.

It all started with a simple question: "What does it truly mean to be an eternal competitor?" The resulting journey has led us to examine some of the most deeply held beliefs that Satan and the world of sports has sold us. We came face to face with the good news of God's unbelievable love and had the opportunity to see exactly where we fit into His story.

We wrestled through joy, failure, identity, freedom from sin, and being a TRUE teammate before taking a firsthand look at what a refined vision can do in the life of a competitor scarred by years of doing it the world's way. We examined and redefined our goal, what it means to win, our audience, and our motivation. Above all, we saw over and over again how the gospel is the eternal thread that weaves its way through every inch of the fabric of life.

It's YOUR time.

Back to *the moment*. It's *your* moment. What will you do with what you now know to be true? My leg of the race is complete, the baton is in your hands, and only you can decide what your next move will be. Unapplied truth is a waste. True life comes from getting in the game and putting it all on the line.

I am praying for you. I am praying that God Himself will give to you the courage and strength to take what He has given to you and put it to work. I am praying that the freedom of the gospel, a freedom like you have never experienced before, would characterize the rest of your days here on Earth. I am praying that, as you fight to put what you have learned into practice, you will remember that the war has already been won and that Jesus' victory will color your every contest. I am praying that the eyes of your heart will always be fixed squarely on the unseen, eternal reality of God's Kingdom running through everything you do. I am praying expectantly for the day when we will all gather in Heaven and rejoice in the innumerable victories God worked in and through us as we walked with Him.

Choose life! Run the race! Fight the fight!

To God be all the glory, all the honor, and all the praise!

Amen.

Therefore we do not lose heart. Though outwardly we are wasting away, yet inwardly we are being renewed day by day. For our light and momentary troubles are achieving for us an eternal glory that far outweighs them all. So we fix our eyes not on what is seen, but on what is unseen, since what is seen is temporary, but what is unseen is eternal.

—2 CORINTHIANS 4:16-18

TRAINING TIME

1. What has God shown you about your relationship with Him? What does it look like to tangibly pursue intimacy with Him?
2. What has God shown you about your view of competition? What is your game plan to stop looking at the temporary things of the world and to start seeing the deeper, eternal elements of your life in the context of sport?
3. What are three specific ways that someone could pray for you as you run the next leg of this race? Who can you share this journey with?